PRAYER
THAT HEALS OUR

D1124822

More praise for *Prayer That Heals Our Emotions*

"This is a must book. . . . The author has had years of experience in teaching Christians how to deepen their prayer life. . . . In a beautifully written book, Ensley leads the Christian through simple exercises designed to activate the imagination into deep, inner healings to experience God's forgiving, compassionate love. He teaches us how to unfold God's hidden powers within our body, soul, and spirit levels to a new dynamic life of intimate love for God and neighbor."
—George Maloney, S.J.

"This remarkable book . . . guides us to a deeper union with God. . . . *Prayer That Heals Our Emotions* takes us on a series of spiritual journeys that lead to an inner peace capable of healing the painful brokeness of the world."
—Judith Lechman, author of *The Spirituality of Gentleness* and *Yielding to Courage*

"This is not just another book on prayer and healing. It is special, unique, and filled with practical wisdom. . . . Ensley's approach to healing opens up the treasures of Christian mystical heritage, a gift so needed in our modern world."
—Rev. Theodore Dobson, author of *Praying for Spiritual Growth*

"I find in this book an unusual balance: it has Biblical and theological integrity; it deals with the self, the others, the world, and thus avoids a form of spirituality that is egocentric and forgets the realities of God's world; it combines strands of Ensley's Protestant background as well as his Roman Catholic piety."
—Neely D. McCarter, Pacific School of Religion

PRAYER
THAT HEALS OUR
Emotions

REVISED *and* EXPANDED EDITION

EDDIE ENSLEY

1817

Harper & Row, Publishers, San Francisco

New York, Grand Rapids, Philadelphia, St. Louis
London, Singapore, Sydney, Tokyo, Toronto

To seven caring friends,
whose love has made this book possible:
Harold McRae, Clair and Jerome Ennis, Judy Esway,
Vicki and Wayne Scheer, and Mary Harris.
And in memory of my cousin, Bill Phelps,
whose goodness touched countless lives.
He was always, for me, my big brother;
and also in memory of Charlie Harris who,
along with his wife Mary,
was so much a part of my beginnings.

"sed ju'beas eam a sanctis angelis su'sciple
et ad patriam paradisi perdu'ci"

FIRST HARPER & ROW EDITION PUBLISHED IN 1988.

Library of Congress Cataloging-in-Publication Data

Ensley, Eddie.
  Prayer that heals our emotions.

  Bibliography: p.
  1. Prayer. 2. Spiritual life—Catholic authors.
3. Spiritual healing. I. Title.
BV215.E57   1988   248.3   88-45134
ISBN 0-06-062253-9

95 96 97 98 RRD H 10 9 8 7 6

CONTENTS

FOREWORD

"Shimmering. Yes, like swimming in moonlight"—that is how the Cherokee Indian, Dane, describes the real world, which is the spiritual world. It is a world that Western people have very little contact with in the modern age. It is lost to the consciousness and desire of most people, except in the fleeting promises of preachers, in the hope awakened by authentic moments of love, and in the now-and-then experience of wondrous awe before grandeur and unfathomability. But even these are not trusted or treasured!

We are a people who have largely defined ourselves outwardly. Within we feel out of control, denied, afraid, guilty, and on foreign soil. We try to compensate by self-help books and courses, by quick aphorisms, and by reliance on the cultural and familial (and untested!) emotional responses. The result is that we are producing the greatest amount of material success along with the greatest amount of neurosis and interpersonal and spiritual failure in the very same group of people. We are educated for careers but not for the living of a full human life. Feelings are not "educated" at all; in fact, most people do not seem to know that it is possible. We must begin.

There is a close and clear connection between our feeling function and our capacity for rich and authentic experience of the Holy. As Abraham Heschel, the Jewish scholar, urgently taught: "The hour calls for a renewal of the antecedents of faith . . . because it is useless to offer conclusions of faith to those who do not have the prerequisites." These necessary "antecedents of faith" are "certain insights, attitudes, and emotions . . . acts that happen within the depth of the person, moments that necessitate groping for faith." It is this rich wellspring of human emotion, where all human motivation, passion, and change begin, that Eddie Ensley seeks to uncover in these prayer exercises.

The Myers-Briggs Personality Profile, which has become well known in church and professional circles, asserts that almost 75 percent of the general population fits into the "sensate" category. This means that the other 25 percent, the "intuitive" types, who have normally written the books of theology, meanings, and explanations, are probably not speaking very well to the mass of the population! Most of the world approaches reality in a hands-on, now, image-oriented way. They are "sensates," who know through experience, detail, memory, through the concrete and the specific. This book is not theoretical at all, but immediately leads the devoted reader to a concrete and image-oriented prayer experience. There is no liberal or conservative theology to argue about, no denominational differences to debate. Eddie just says, "Let's pray and let God's action and presence speak for itself!" In that sense it is a risky and demanding book, a wonderful book.

After sixteen years on the road preaching myself, and fourteen years as pastor of a lay community, I am painfully aware of how difficult it is to form people in a holistic relationship to the gospel. Some want prayer meetings, some want Scripture study, some want service and ministry, some want education, and some want consolation. Others want to be prophetic to the system, while others believe that religion is an inner affair of healing and personal wholeness. The health of this book is that all aspects of our life and the gospel call are presented for consideration and healing. How good to see a book that can talk about inner healing, contemplation, sexual lovemaking, and nuclear disarmament under the same cover! These are signs of a maturing and adult Christianity that is unfolding in our time, despite all the annoying evidence to the contrary. "For where sin abounds, there grace abounds even more," says St. Paul (Rom. 5:20).

May grace abound through these words and prayers—"yes, like swimming in moonlight"—the shimmering real world!

Richard Rohr, O.F.M.

PREFACE TO THE REVISED EDITION

During the spring and summer of 1987, I fell in love with Scripture for a second time. For the first time in years, I had time to spend many hours a week with the Bible, letting it become fuel for meditation. Scripture bathed me and cradled me with a sense of how safe it is to be in God's presence. This time I was secure and strong enough to feel and let go of some of my most entrenched pain.

Right along with my second honeymoon with the Bible, I discovered the writings of biblical scholar Walter Brueggemann. His penetrating and poetic insights into Scripture gave me language to understand what had been going on inside my heart for the last several years. Brueggemann shows how Scripture calls us to grieve over our hurts and the hurts of our wounded world. The Bible amply supplies us with imagery and symbols to feel our hurts, and it rescues us from the prevailing numbness of our society. But Scripture does not just leave us with our hurts; it energizes us with amazement and hope—the sort of hope that we could not manufacture or invent but is a gift that comes from beyond us.

As my heart was being refreshed by this experience, I found myself wishing that all these insights had blossomed in me when I wrote and self-published the first edition of this book in 1986. I had no idea how soon my prayer would be answered. I was startled by one of those bright surprises that now and then erupt into our lives. The phone rang, and an editor was calling to ask if Harper & Row could publish a new edition of *Prayer That Heals Emotions.* He also asked if I wanted to add any new material. After several days of reflection, I said a strong yes to both questions.

When the time came to begin the revisions, I found myself in the midst of a creative whirlwind. By the time it subsided, I had two hundred typed pages in hand, more than the original book and far too much material. So I spent the next few weeks cutting, editing, and merging the new material with the first edition. In doing this, I more than doubled the number of guided meditations in the book.

By far the most important new materials are the biblical meditations that I have added to most chapters. I call them Scripture Journeys, and they ground personal prayer in our common scriptural heritage. Nearly as important are the stories from my own and others' experiences—the many accounts of our prayers, suffering, love, and hope. Jesus could not talk without telling a story; stories are the keys that open the padlocked rooms in our hearts.

Many thanks to all the readers who have written to me to share their journeys and their hearts. Please continue to write.

Eddie Ensley
February 1988

ACKNOWLEDGMENTS

This book was completed during a time of family tragedy. One close relative died suddenly and unexpectedly; another was killed in an automobile accident that critically injured another relative. In the midst of the pain and grief I drew closer to my family, especially my parents. My father's manly tenderness and gentleness have healed and sustained me all my life. My mother's strength, understanding, and ferocious ability to love and care are treasures I cherish. And the courage of my Aunt Margaret and my cousin Gay Phelps, as well as my aunt, Genella Crittenden, in the midst of loss is a deep inspiration.

PART ONE

Tools for Transformation

HEALING THE HURT PLACES

As I was being introduced, I clung tightly to a quarter in my pocket. Rubbing its rough edges against my fingers seemed to reduce my tension slightly. Like most speakers, I am always a little tense before I speak; I believe they call it preperformance anxiety. This time it overwhelmed me.

One of the members of the diocesan renewal committee that had invited us to do the retreat, a young family practice physician named Kate, had greeted me with scarcely veiled skepticism and hostility at supper. "Don't you think meditation should remain in the monasteries? I've always been taught that meditation is for the very advanced. And here you are telling us about teenagers, housewives, and mechanics entering into the same prayer experiences the spiritual masters wrote about."

Her words had stung, and I let them throw me off balance. I was about to give the first session of a weekend retreat designed to lead people into deep inner peace and healing, even though at that moment my heart was far from peaceful.

I looked down into the audience at Kate's sterile, antiseptic expression that scarcely masked her skepticism and anger. I stumbled through the first few sentences, then realized I couldn't finish the talk. I moved on to the guided prayer experience, playing a slow version of Bach's "Jesu" on the stereo system as soft background to the meditation. As I paused in the stillness I realized one more time that it was not my words or style or knowledge of theology that would bring healing, but God's all-feeling compassion and love. We were just providing the spiritual and emotional space for people to open up to that love.

As I began to enter into the quiet myself, my anxiety receded. I felt a loving and warming energy pour over me as if I were in a shower of light. I sensed others entering that shower of light with me. Tears softly coursed down people's faces. A calmness thick with warmth and love came over us, knitting our hearts together. It was as though in the silence we were now breathing one breath and experiencing the reality that one Heart beats in all of us. I gently and slowly continued the meditations, leading the group in remembering past joys and imagining a scene from Scripture.

Toward the end of the prayer experience, I noticed Kate, the young doctor, sobbing. Hers were not the shallow, tight, frantic sobs that come from hopelessness but the deep purifying sobs that come from finally letting loose deeply entrenched pain. After we finished the session, Kate took me aside and told me her story, letting me know what had happened to her during the prayer experience.

Her mother had died of cancer when Kate was eight. In his grief, her father had become more and more dependent on Kate, his only child, for emotional nurture, asking for an adult love that no little girl is capable of giving. As his drinking habit developed into alcoholism, he abused her first with violent words then with violent actions. She showed me a scar on her hand from a cigarette burn and another above her eye from a belt buckle. A crash into a bridge abutment killed her father when she was eleven, after which a loving aunt reared her and sent her through school.

The shock, the scars of what had happened to her bored into the center of her being. Deep inside her heart she blamed herself for her father's death. Her emotions shut down, her personality became rigid. If only she had loved him enough, she had always thought.

She then told me what happened during the prayer experience: "I felt an injection of love warming my heart, warming my body. When you asked us to remember joyful times, I went back to the time before my mother got sick. I saw the three of us happy, laughing, enjoying homemade ice cream on the back porch. We were happy then. In that memory, for the first time in my adult life, I felt my daddy's love. I know he cared for me, cherished me. He just couldn't handle Mother's death. I felt grief and pain too, grief that he is gone, grief that he didn't recover. The hurt and the grief I felt as we prayed were immense, but the sense of love and caring was even greater."

Kate continued the journey that began during the retreat. She started seeing a Christian psychotherapist so that the healing would continue. She initiated a daily program of healing meditation. When I saw her next, the hostility that had covered shame had been replaced by a gentleness and strength that drew from the wellsprings of her being.

Loved Deep Within

How much useless energy is spent digging for painful memories when the real hunger is for loving affirmation—affirmation that allows the hurt we cannot reach with all our searching and willing to come to the surface. The deeper levels of our psyches won't let go of the tightly guarded hurt, the deepest memories, until confronted with love and nurture strong enough to replace the hurt. Then, the inward parts of us that clutch so tightly to pain begin to trust and let go.

Many of the prayer experiences we use in this book and on our retreats are designed to feed our deeper selves with affirmations—affirmations of God's love, affirmations of the essential wholeness of each of us. The prayer experiences instill hope, but not the shallow kind of hope that suggests we can avoid reality by thinking "nice" thoughts. The prayer experiences bring hope by filling the inner recesses of our being with the central reality of faith—that we are created by a loving God who sent his Son to redeem us. We are grasped by God's affirmation. We experience his love at the very heart of things, a love that cannot and will not let us go. And that love makes all things fresh and new.

When we open our hearts wide to God's caring the deeper roots of our nature find the permanent soil of an infinite love. We find in the cellars of our souls an ocean of infinite rest that gives meaning to our seemingly endless activities. There is a place within where the sea is always calm and the boats are steady, and Christian meditation takes our awareness to that place. The kingdom of God, Jesus said, is within us.

When we enter into depth prayer we are taken into the arms of a God who will never forsake us from his embrace. As we surrender ourselves to the power of Another, to something greater than ourselves, a force is mobilized within that helps affirm our goodness and wholeness.

Yet many of us fear this opening to love. We know that as we relax our guard and let love in we will feel the hurts we spend so much energy trying not to feel, and we fear these feelings will overwhelm us. But like Kate's experience, and like many others I have known, when our guard relaxes because love has touched us, it goes down at just the right pace. Our pain didn't come in an instant and our healing doesn't come in an instant. Real and lasting healing resembles the gentle and gradual changing of seasons, rather than an overpowering summer thunderstorm.

We may never discover the origin of some of our pain, and that's okay. We don't always need to know where it came from to let it go. Romans 8 tells us that when we do not know how to pray, the Spirit prays through us with sighs too deep for words. Each of us is a fathomless depth and only God can know us fully. In meditation we give the Holy Spirit permission to search those depths. As our healing unfolds, we will find that at times a hurt is welling up inside and we don't know why. When that happens, we can grieve and weep and let go of our grip. This is what I believe Paul meant by sighs too deep for words.

Over a period of time, as prayer deepens the work of healing in our lives, a deep joy will root itself in the wellsprings of our being. The sunshine will appear to have more splendor and we shall be able to feel the warmth of words expressed by others rather than suspect ill will hidden in them. We learn to drink in the beauty of each present moment. The trees, the stars and blue hills, the touch of another human being appear to us as symbols aching with a meaning that can never be uttered in words. Nature begins to reflect the eternal. Water does more than wash our limbs; it brightens our hearts. The earth we walk on does more than hold our bodies; it gladdens our minds, transmitting to our being the maternal tenderness of God.

2

WHAT IS HEALING
MEDITATION?

How can I draw close to God? This is a question that all of us ask. At times it throbs like a toothache. At other times it lies buried beneath the clutter of everyday busyness. But the question remains always with us.

We yearn to draw close to God because there have been special grace-filled times in all our lives when the mysterious at-homeness of his love caressed and enveloped us. Such times usually sneak up on us unexpectedly. Perhaps you are running along the beach. You cease to be aware of the movement of your muscles, or the splashing of your feet in the sand. The sound of the breaking waves stills and calms your mind. You seem one with the sea, the beach—you feel connected. Your fears leave you for a moment. You do not think of God; you experience him. He seems closer to you than the blood that surges through your veins. From the cellar of your soul you call him Father.

Or perhaps such a "close encounter" comes as you tenderly touch and reverence the skin of your spouse in the midst of the marriage kiss. Maybe it occurs in the unexpected sense of love and peace you feel in the midst of tragedy, when the person you thought would never leave you lies in a cool metal box awaiting burial. Such times come in traditional ways too, while you are reading the Bible, receiving communion, or voicing your praise. These times tantalize us, tease us, make us hungry for more. They put us in touch with dimensions of our life that are missing, parts of ourselves we knew were there all along but had lost contact with.

This book presents practical pathways to growing close to God and becoming whole, ways so simple and so obvious that we easily overlook them. Learning Christian meditation will be an adventure, the adventure of discovering who you really are and loving who you really are. And as you increasingly open your heart to the love of God in meditation, you will more and more learn to love the people around you. A fresh joy will root itself deep in the cellar of your soul. As the new love and life within you help you to spend yourself for God, others, and the poor, you can begin to say with St. Paul "It is not I who live but Christ who lives within me" (Gal. 2:20).

OPENING DOORS

Some things defy easy definition. No one definition or even a thousand definitions come close to describing God or love or hope. We sing, tell stories, paint pictures with words to get at realities that are larger than life.

So it is with meditation. In working on this book I searched for a word-picture, story, or image that would describe meditation. Although I ran scores of images through the slide projector of my mind, I couldn't find one that by itself would convey the reality of meditation. I soon found that a number of different metaphors are needed.

One especially vivid picture description is based on an early memory. My mind returns to the simple white-stucco house my Cherokee grandparents rented from the cotton mill where they worked. The first thing I saw every time I entered their tiny living room was a faded and sentiment-filled picture of Jesus, staff in hand, knocking on the door of a house. The door was special; it had no outside latch. Under the picture was a written explanation. It said that Jesus stood at the door of our hearts knocking, but that he would not barge in or open the door himself. He was gentle; he respected our freedom. He wanted to be invited in. The latch was on the inside of our hearts. We could decide to let him in. The picture quoted the words of the King James Bible: "Behold, I stand at the door and knock. If any man hear my voice and open up to me, I will come in and sup with him and he with me" (Rev. 3:20).

For me this old painting is an apt description of Christian meditation. In Christian meditation we unlatch the doors of our hearts so Christ can fill us with his gospel and his love. And we open the door to him not once but countless times. Our hearts have many doors and many rooms. The art of Christian meditation is the art of learning to open those doors to the endless beauty of our Eternal Lover.

Meditation is prayer that sinks below the surface of conscious thought. This is much of what is meant by the phrase "praying with our whole hearts." The concept of the subconscious is accepted by almost everyone today. Our minds are often compared to icebergs. Only the smaller part of an iceberg protrudes above the surface. So it is with our consciousness; the larger part, the real us, lies below the surface. Here are stored old memories, good and bad, the fresh bright wonderful memories of early childhood, and traumas buried so deep we wall them off from awareness. Here resides our sexuality. Here is the buried sublimity of our higher self as well as the cesspool of our darkness. Meditation is letting prayer sink to these hidden parts.

Scripture speaks of these depths: "For the inward mind and heart of a man are deep!" (Ps. 64:6B). "For he knows the secrets of the heart" (Ps. 44:21). "The Lord sees not as man sees; man looks on the outwards appearance, but the Lord looks on the heart" (1 Sam. 16:7). "The Lord searches all hearts, and understands every plan and thought" (1 Chron. 28:9).

Motivational researcher Anne White in *Healing Adventure* summed up this need for the transformation of our subconscious: "If your faith is grounded in the subconscious mind, it will sustain you through any crisis. If it is no deeper than your conscious mind, it will desert you in the moment you are off guard.

Its God-given power is amazing. Jesus Christ knew all about the subconscious mind and the part it played in our lives."

Despite the profound interest in meditation our modern culture has developed recently, we are an outward-turned, extroverted society. We are not at home with inner silence, with our inner selves. That is why we run from solitude as quickly as we run from a mugger. Yet when we open the inner doors to God's unfathomable love, we find healing for our deepest wounds and the release of a whirlwind of strength for creative loving and creative living.

How easy it is for our prayer to stay on the surface. Surface prayer is more like dictation than conversation. It tends to be a one-way monologue. We tell God what we want him to do, ask him to bless our plans, and then go merrily on our way. St. Catherine of Siena, that feisty, fiery, loving woman of prayer who lived in the fourteenth century, summed up this attitude. She was once asked why God no longer conversed with people in the familiar personal way he did in times past. She answered, "God is no longer as personal as He once was because instead of treating Him as the Master and seeing ourselves as the disciple, we treat Him as the disciple and act like we are the Master."

In short, instead of praying, "Speak Lord, your servant is listening," we pray, "Listen Lord, your servant is speaking."

THE SPECIAL DIFFERENCE

Meditation gets top billing today. Even some corporations have set aside special meditation rooms for their top executives, hoping this will help these executives avoid heart attacks. Meditation is in. It lowers blood pressure, prevents disease, reduces stress, helps your sex life, and improves your golf score—so the talk shows and popular magazines tell us. And they are right. Secular meditation does bring some of these benefits. So does Christian meditation.

What, then, makes Christian meditation different? Love!

That's what makes the difference. The core of Christian meditation is love: loving God, loving yourself, loving people, loving the whole world. As Augustine put it, "True, whole prayer is nothing but love."

Christian meditation at its heart is not just a great set of benefits. Yes, the benefits are there but they are secondary. All Christian prayer goes beyond the category of usefulness, beyond an enhanced ability to play a better tennis game or get more out of jogging. It offers nothing less than a fiery and eternal love affair with the passionate and all-compassionate Lover who dances throughout the cosmos and in the bosom of our own hearts. Christianity stands under the shadow of a personal God. We believe in a God who cares, who is active in the world, the Yahweh who weaves his way through the story of ancient Israel, the story of Jesus, and the personal stories of each of us.

Meditation is a powerful interchange of love with God in the cellar of our souls. It is as St. Bonaventure so strikingly put it "the fire that totally inflames us and carries us into God" till we become "inflamed in the very marrow by the fire of the Holy Spirit." In Christian meditation, we open up the inner passageways of our core being and allow this Passionate One of Israel, the God of Jesus, to express his love to us.

All prayer, all meditation begins with God's action toward us. Meditation is taking a sunbath in his caring, "an inner bath of love into which the soul plunges itself," as St. Jean Vianney put it. In meditation we allow God to love us.

The Whole of Us

Christianity is the earthiest religion. It takes this world very seriously. "God so loved the world that he gave his only Son" (John 3:16).

There is no special spiritual section inside us barricaded from the rest of us. God wants to involve each particle of our being, down to the cells of our fingernails, in our love affair with him.

So Christian meditation involves not just our religious side. Our sexuality, our bodies, our intellects, our relationships with others, our work, all become part of our meditation.

It is not so much that we pray as that we *become* a prayer. An early biographer of St. Francis, Thomas Celano, describes how Francis gave his whole self over to God in prayer: "All his attention and affection he directed with his *whole being* . . . to the Lord, not so much praying as becoming himself a prayer." So it should be with us.

This book will carry you on a journey into meditation. Some of the themes of the prayer experiences may at first not seem particularly religious. They include personal relationships, the healing of past hurts, and learning how to love. This is because God is concerned with all of us and when we pray, when we meditate, we present all of ourselves to him.

The journey deeper into God's love hurts. It is not just a fresh high. In falling in love with anyone there is pain. We go through a healing process in meditation. We open up the different rooms of our hearts to Christ and he sweeps them clean, then gets out the mop and scrubs away the encrusted grime. So there are times we must look at the grime and together with God take care of it. This is no lark. Facing the grunge inside of us hurts. Lawrence LeShan in *How to Meditate* quotes Nikos Kazantzakis describing this decision to yield to God's cleansing, healing therapy: "God is fire and you must walk on it . . . dance on it. At that moment the fire will become cool water. But until you reach that point, what a struggle, my Lord, what agony!"

Loving What God Loves[*]

Francis of Assisi once said, years after he had begun his meditative journey, that the things he formerly despised were now sweet to him and the things he once loved he now disliked.

When you fall in love with someone, your likes begin to change. You begin to love the things that person loves. We first of all begin to love other Christians. The New Testament says that we know that we have passed from death to life when we begin to love fellow believers. We realize that we are on this journey with others—with friends, with family, with the Church.

Meditation is not a solitary, introspective, belly-gazing experience. There is an outward movement in meditation as well as an inward movement. We seek an ongoing involvement with brothers and sisters. We begin to love and serve the poor as Jesus loves and serves the poor. We become deeply involved in living out our love relationship in everyday life—loving God in those around us. We realize that the whole of the cosmos groans, like us, for completion.

SCRIPTURE JOURNEY*

Behold, I stand at the door and knock; if any one hears my voice and opens the door, I will come in to him and eat with him, and he with me. He who conquers, I will grant him to sit with me on my throne, as I myself conquered and sat down with my Father on his throne

(REV. 3:20–21).

Take some time to enter into the ease of deep relaxation. Put on some soothing instrumental music. Allow yourself to enter into a deep calm. We will be inviting Jesus into the depths of our unconscious life and in doing so, we will say a deeper yes to him. If you have difficulty imagining this scene, skip ahead to chapter 5 and then return to this meditation.

You are out in the woods, and in front of you is a hill, on the side of which you see the entrance to a cave; a door blocks your passage. The cave symbolizes your unconscious, your deep heart. There reside bright gifts, learnings, parts of yourself that are rich and vital and that you have forgotten or that have fallen asleep; gifts that

*The first part of this meditation is adapted from *Prayer, Stress, and Our Inner Wounds,* Flora S. Wuellner (Nashville: Upper Room, 1985).

have never been given, a diamond mine of sparkling gems.

Also locked away down there are the children of your pain, as Flora Wuellner has called them: the children that you once were, the children that were once hurt and "have been buried so deeply down inside that you can't hear their crying anymore." Deep inside you, too, are the healthy children that you once were, alive and vibrant.

As you look at the entrance of the cave, you sense someone walking up behind you. It is Jesus. He places his hand on your shoulder and you feel the peace that his touch brings. Jesus will be entering this cave and going down into its depths to comfort the hurting children. You are not to go down with him, but you walk to the door and open it for Jesus. As he descends into the depths, you stay outside the cave door, praying for him. Down inside, he is embracing the wounded children in long, lingering, tender embraces, cradling them, comforting them, enfolding them in a total love, a pure love. He wipes away their tears.

After a long time, you hear Jesus coming back up. When he opens the door, an immense, radiant light pours from the cave. In his hand is a beautiful diamond that sparkles with intense brightness. You immediately sense the meaning of this diamond. It is a part of you that has been there all along, hidden away from your consciousness. Jesus walks toward you and presses it into your hand with the palm of his hand. You feel the healing flow up through your arm. As you clutch it tightly, an incredible power rushes through your body. As the diamond merges with your hand, a vast brightness fills your whole body. Somehow you know that in the upcoming days and weeks, you will discover the significance of this gift in the midst of your daily living. A new talent, a new ability to love, a new enthusiasm may begin to burst forth in you.

Jesus goes back down again. You can hear the sounds of laughter and joy and fun from inside the cave. Jesus is playing with the children you once were. They are healthy, vibrant children. He also plays with the children that he comforted, that are on their way to being healed. After a while, you hear him coming up. He walks out the door, bringing with him one of the healthy children, one of the children who is spontaneous and loves fun. What is your reaction on seeing that child, that child that you once were? Jesus introduces the happy child to the adult you. Play with that child for a while. How does it feel to play? Just enjoy yourself. When you are finished, take the child in your arms. You will find that the child merges with you, flowing into you. Joyousness and wonder flow throughout your body. You suspect that in the next few days you'll be looking out on this world with a fresh, childlike wonder; a new playfulness, a new lightness, a new ease will come into your life.

3

IMAGINATION—A DOORWAY TO THE HEART

Gregg lived in a world of books, a world that had little room for people. In the inner chamber of his heart, he suffered the most painful ache a human being can suffer, the ache of loneliness.

For fifteen years he had taught Latin at a prep school. A faithful churchgoer, he came to our seminar. He came because he had read some of the theological research I had done in historical spirituality. He thought the seminar would be primarily on the theological plane. When I noticed him in the crowd, he looked much younger than his thirty-six years. His back was stone rigid in the foldout chair. I think he was genuinely surprised when my first talk was about our emotions and how to draw personally close to God, rather than an exposition on theology. Our seminar was aimed at helping people open up the passageways of their hearts to the love of one another, to God's love, and to the call of the gospel.

I noticed his barely disguised grimaces at some of the personal stories I was telling. Each time the talk touched on emotions, he would roll his eyes or lean back. In the question-and-answer period, it became clear that he wanted to spar with me. He did not so much ask questions as give short little speeches. One of his opening lines was, "I doubt that St. Thomas Aquinas would completely agree with the definition of love you gave." He then quoted Aquinas briefly in Latin and translated it himself. His attempt to impress everyone was painfully obvious. I saw some of the people in the group straining to keep from laughing. A few passed knowing looks to one another. They had known him for years.

After each meeting Gregg would grab me, spouting this or that quote from church fathers. He seemed desperately to need my approval. But he never said anything personal about himself; in fact, he didn't show an ounce of emotion the whole weekend. It seemed as though he could not talk without uttering a footnote. Normally I would have said, "Please, I need a few minutes to get my thoughts together for the next talk." But as distracting as he was, I felt that I needed to give him this time.

Several months after the seminar, I was very surprised to receive a phone call from Gregg. He sounded like a different person. It was obvious that he was trying to speak through sobs and tears. "I'm so alone, so very alone." His words continued to be interrupted by sobs as his story emerged in our conversation. He had picked up more of what we were saying at the retreat than he had let on then. With the same diligence that he brought to his studies and teaching, he had gone through my book and started listening to guided prayer journeys on tape. Nothing seemed to happen at first, but he persisted and finally over several weeks, he felt the hurt emerging in his being. Finally, it flooded out and overflowed—the ache of loneliness, the ache of not having anyone with whom to share, even more than that, the ache of not knowing how to share, how to reach out, or how to be open to receive or to give love.

"I don't know how to love," he said. I listened and then told him, "Gregg, you have just loved me. You loved me more deeply than I could tell you by this phone conversation. You trusted me enough to share some of the deep-down hurt in your heart. Your trust is a way of loving me. You've taken your guts in your hands, presented them to me, and risked rejection. You have loved me tonight."

A mellowness came into his voice, a softness that I had not heard on the retreat. I prayed with him that night. In subsequent phone conversations, it became clear that Gregg had embarked on the slow process of learning how to share himself. He began to open up to one of the associate pastors at his church. He joined one of the sharing groups. Sometimes he would sound joyful; at other times there would be pain in his voice. But I rejoiced that he had finally discovered his emotions. He had used prayer and imagination to uncover the pain imprisoned in his depths. I just know in my heart that he is going to flower into a full person. I wouldn't be surprised if a couple of years from now I get a wedding invitation from him. I know he faces a long and rough journey, but I know too that he will be taking that journey with people who love him and with a God who is constantly knocking at the doors of his heart, offering love and healing. This is one of many examples I have seen of how meditation can open the way for love, a way for newness to bud forth in our lives.

A research project of the great psychoanalyst Carl Jung took him to the American Southwest, where he interviewed the famous Pueblo chief Ochwraybiano. The doctor asked the Indian what he thought of white men. "Not much," replied the chief. "They're always restless, upset, looking for something more. That's why their faces are wrinkled."

He went on to say that white people must be crazy because they think with their heads: "And only crazy people think with their heads." "Then how do the Indians think?" asked Jung. "With their hearts, of course," answered the old chief.

One of the greatest tragedies of modern culture is that we think mostly with our heads. We leave out our hearts, our inner core. As a result, our world is fragmented, partial; things just don't "come together," to use a modern phrase. Meditation, in large part, means learning to think, to pray, to experience again with our hearts. We don't abandon thinking with our heads; we bring head and heart together. We become whole.

How do you begin to pray, to think with the heart? You begin by using the language of the heart, the language of imagination. Modern psychologists and scientists are rediscovering what many of the more "together" cultures before us knew instinctively—that the language of the subconscious is the language of images, symbols, imagination. As Frances E. Vaughan in *Awakening Intuition* has written:

Imagery is the universal language of the unconscious. Thinking in pictures precedes thinking in words. Imagery is associated with direct perception and conveys in an instant feelings and observations which would take many words to describe.

This explains why the language of Scripture is full of imagery, symbolism, story. The Scriptures speak to the whole person, both head and heart. They speak of God with such evocative imagery that they usher us into his presence.

The biblical scholar Amos Wilder in *Theopoetic* wrote that the use of imagination is the dominant characteristic in the message of Jesus: "The hearer not only learns about that reality, he participates in it. He is invaded by it. . . . Jesus' speech had the character not of instruction and ideas but of *compelling imagination,* a spell, . . . a transformation." Just look at some of the images Jesus used: a candle covered by a bushel basket, pearls thrown before swine, fishermen with a dragnet pulling in unimaginable varieties of fish, people digging up treasure in a field.

I think it's important here to talk about some of the differences between "head" thinking and "heart" thinking. Just because heart thinking plays such a vital role in our becoming whole doesn't mean that we should neglect rational thinking. To be complete we need to use both ways of experiencing the world. We need to blend head and heart together.

Most of us are used to rational thinking, linear logical thinking. Many researchers associate logical thinking with the left side of the brain. Intuitive, imaginative, creative thinking is centered in the right side of the brain. As one friend put it: "With the logical part of us we comprehend and understand ideas about God; with the intuitive part of us we apprehend and experience him."

In *Directing the Movies of Your Mind,* Adelaide Bry and Marjorie Bair use a striking illustration that shows the difference in the two ways of thinking. A freight train passes rapidly down the track and there are two people watching it. One person standing three feet from the track as the train goes by sees what is passing directly in front of him—the engine, one car at a time, and then the caboose. This is much how the logical side of the brain operates, taking one thing at a time. Now let's imagine another person. This person looks at the train from high above it, floating in a balloon. Instead of seeing one car or one part of a car at a time, he sees the total train, as well as the surrounding country-side. This is "holistic" experiencing, experiencing that takes in the whole.

Imaginative thinking is nonrational. This doesn't mean irra-tional. It means that it goes beyond the rational, penetrates deeper than the rational. What we are saying, in short, is that the old saying, "A picture is worth a thousand words," is profoundly true.

Phrases from Scripture such as "The Word became a human being and dwelt among us" and "I am the Light of the World" do not make strict logical sense. They are nonrational, yet they convey realities and truths a thousand books could not convey. These are examples of powerful "holistic" thinking. They take us high in a hot air balloon and let us see the whole landscape in one glance.

IMAGINATION—A FORGOTTEN ART

Our modern society has lost touch with how to use the imagi-nation. And it's killing us. Imagination once functioned as a means of evoking religious experience. Words conveyed pictures that would evoke the experience of God. In the last centuries we have lived in an abstract and labeled world, a world in which words no longer have the same ability to usher us into experience. This bleaches us of much of our humanity. It deprives us of much of our ability to experience God.

Physicians and researchers are finding bright new horizons in the healing of people's bodies and psyches through the use of relaxation and imagination. Case after case, study after study show the profound truth of psychotherapists Adelaide Bry and Marjorie Bair's observation that "At a practical level, visualization has an uncanny ability to improve the quality of our lives. It does this through its power to heal the body and spirit, to reconstruct the past, and to reveal our hidden truths . . . the most dramatic visualizations touch the deepest part of ourselves, our essence, our core—and allow us to experience connections beyond ourselves."

Pain control centers such as the UCLA Pain Control Center, directed by Dr. David E. Bressler, and the Health Rehabilitation Center in Wisconsin, directed by Dr. C. Norman Shealy, are pioneering new directions. Patients come to these centers, often with migraine headaches or pain from back injuries that no amount of sedation will cure or relieve. By use of a combination of relaxation, imagination, and meditation, Dr. Shealy has found that 72 percent of his patients have at least 50 percent improvement, and of those, at least half experience from 90 to 100 percent relief.

Imagination has a profound healing effect not only on the body but on the emotions as well. Dr. David Schultz obtained some remarkable results with depressed patients at the Westhaven VA Hospital in Connecticut. He divided these patients into two groups. One group he encouraged to use positive fantasies or daydreams, such as picturing themselves in a beautiful field or receiving compliments from someone who admired them. The other group was just encouraged to let daydreams come as they would without directing them or handling them in any way. Those directed into fantasies of beautiful nature scenes and of people affirming them showed remarkable improvement in their depression. Dr. Schultz later tried these methods with healthy individuals and found that nature scenes and other healing images helped improve their moods when they were depressed and blue. Numerous other counselors have had excellent results helping normal people cope with life and better fulfill their potential. All this points to the powerful impact our imaginations have upon both our emotions and our bodies.

The experience of physicians and researchers in using the imagination to heal is simply rediscovery of what the writers of Scripture and many of the great figures of Christian tradition knew all along. Christian use of the imagination in prayer can carry us even further than these modern psychotherapeutic rediscoveries. "Grace," St. Thomas says, "builds upon the natural." Christian use of the imagination can put us in touch with God, the God of love whose touch brings wholeness.

4

IMAGINATION—A WAY OF PRAYER

The three of us were on our way to southern Louisiana "Cajun" country to conduct two weeks of retreats and seminars. As our little Datsun churned its way through the icy February rain, the center of my chest ached with anxiety and apprehension. I felt inadequate—physically, emotionally, and spiritually—for the tasks that awaited me in Louisiana.

Several weeks earlier in an emergency operation that saved my life, a surgeon had taken out my acutely infected gallbladder. I was really not ready for such an exhausting mission, and the doctor had only reluctantly given me permission for the trip.

The day we set out, my winter cold turned into a nasty bronchitis. I was in such a haze from my physical condition that putting two coherent sentences together took effort. Pictures of my stammering in front of the audiences passed through my mind. I had no idea what I was going to say. The first engagement concerned me the most. I was supposed to lead a day of recollection for a group of four hundred young people aged thirteen through twenty-three from Lafayette diocesan youth groups.

One of my coworkers, Pat Bartholomew, a young man whose eyes glisten with vitality and determination, picked up the worry in my face. With a half-smile he said, "Eddie, here's a time I can remind you of some of the advice you give other people. God can use you most when you are at your weakest. You've been telling people lately how by using the imagination in prayer we can become channels for God's love. Here's a time for you to try it."

I took up his challenge. My hazy mind began to go over

scenes in Scripture that involve healing light imagery. My mind turned to the lowly young girl Mary who opened her heart wide enough to receive the light of God at the annunciation. I remembered the scene of James and John standing in awe at the light of the transfiguration and Saul knocked off his horse by the blinding light of God's presence.

I visualized a large ray of soothing, healing light beaming down on me as I sat in the little Datsun seat. I allowed that light to energize me, comfort me, heal me, and tell me of God's love in a way deeper than words. Every time my mind wandered away, I returned to the image of myself sitting under the light of God's presence.

That night as I lay in bed awaiting sleep the picture prayer changed. The light not only surrounded me but went through my hands and heart. It went out from me and surrounded others. I pictured the whole gym full of young people inundated in the light of God's love.

The next day with the four hundred young people became the bright spot of our whole year of retreats. I don't remember what I said. My mind was still foggy; my chest still ached. But I felt a great love from beyond myself surge through me as I spoke. I remember leading them through some of the meditations I used in my own prayer. By the end of the day many were in tears, they were so deeply touched. A score or more asked to take the microphone and share a little of what had happened in their hearts that day. Some as young as thirteen told how their faith came alive for them for the first time. One muscular young man of twenty, a former linebacker for LSU who had dropped out of football because of a knee injury, came forward. His eyes moist with tears, he told how he had been afraid to be weak and transparent. That day he had learned the power of not pretending. He said he wanted his friends to be Christian friends; he was choosing a Christian life-style.

As I drove away that evening I was reconvinced that God works best through our weakness. But in a way that goes beyond just the natural, it also enabled more of me to become a channel of a light and a healing love that was beyond myself. I was saying a yes with my subconscious as well as my conscious mind.

PROGRAMMED IMAGINATION IN PRAYER

Programmed imagination in prayer is when we actively set up certain scenes to imagine. The symbols, stories, and images of Scripture provide hundreds of starting places. Such visualizations help deepen our sense of God's loving us. Such active imagination is dosing ourselves with the gospel. We begin to center our personalities around gospel symbols and gospel pictures. We open doors for God's message of love in the bosom of our souls.

Recently I had great difficulty working on some of my writing projects. I had a classic case of writer's block. Sitting at the typewriter and staring at a blank page every day took big chunks out of my self-image. Then I began to let it be a matter of prayer. I thanked God for his love for me. I told him that I recognized that he loved me whether or not I worked on my book and articles. Then I said, "Lord, I know you have called me to write. Help me with my writing."

I pictured finished manuscripts. I pictured myself thumbing through the pages while surrounded by the light of God's love. I imagined some of my friends saying, "This material really touched me to the heart. It really helped me love the poor; it helped put me in contact with God." Then I saw myself doing the tasks that were involved in writing—taking notes, typing, dictating.

There was no overnight miracle. But I daily used this picture prayer when I asked God to help me with my writing. Such prayer bolstered and strengthened my inner self. The energies and abilities found deep in me were marshaled to the task before me. It took several weeks, but then I suddenly found myself flooded with ideas. The discipline that had seemed so hard now seemed easy. I organized my tasks daily and the material began to pour out. I finished pages a day rather than just a few paragraphs. Many who read the material were touched. I had experienced the power of picture prayer.

Robert, my co-worker in our small apostolate who has a profound, simple spirituality, wanted very much for his life to be in touch with the poor. Although we live a simple life-style in a poor neighborhood, we are invited to speak all over the world and the people who invite us take us to the fanciest restaurants, the nicest clubs, the nicest beaches. Living a life of simplicity and poverty was important for us at that time, but because a large part of our apostlate is reaching out, helping to renew parishes and give retreats, we were not home year-round to develop a steady ministry to the poor. We knew we needed the poor in our lives, not just for their sakes but for ours. We needed the grace of God that comes through the poor, because the poor are so close to him.

Robert especially began to pray daily that God would help him in knowing how to love the poor and let the poor love him. He prayed the Scripture with his imagination, "Inasmuch as you have done it to the least of these, my brethren, you have done it unto me" (Matt. 25:40, KJV). He pictured himself loving and being loved by different types of poor people.

Then, after weeks of this, some of our elderly neighbors, some on food stamps, one who had suffered a debilitating stroke, another whose wife had died, began coming to us spontaneously, just to be around us. Robert especially took time for them, sitting with them on the porch, taking them to lunch and for rides, just being someone to help take away their loneliness. He started having lunch with an old man who supplemented his $200-a-month Social Security income by gathering aluminum cans from trash bins in the park.

Robert spends a great deal of time with friends like these whose need is obvious. And they have been a great joy to him; God's love has come to him in beautiful ways through them. His picture prayer brought him into contact with the poor. His picture prayer helped him begin to live the gospel. Most of us don't have the same intense vocation to be involved with the poor that Robert has. But each of us according to his or her own calling in life can use imaginative prayer to bolster our decision to live the Gospels in our own life situation.

Gospel Commercials

Imaginative prayer is a window to self-knowledge. In imagination we can dose ourselves with gospel commercials. Commercials on television, radio, and in the movies know this technique of imagination. Some car commercials use powerful, cosmic, magical religious symbolism as well as sexy girls, all pointing out the wonders of some new sports car. They know the route to the core of us. These commercials tell us that our salvation, our wholeness, comes in consuming and buying more and more. They lie to us.

To counteract their muddy, murky message we need to give ourselves daily gospel commercials. We need to use the truths and power of the messages of Scripture and Christian tradition to fill our inner selves with powerful and strengthening images. We need images that heal us and help us to know the power of God's love, help us to open the deepest doors of our heart to the penetrating light of that love. These images help us to know that we are like babies in our Father's arms: we know his caresses, his loving caring, his tenderness. They lead us to spend ourselves in serving and loving others. We begin to integrate our personalities around these images.

IMAGINATION IN SCRIPTURE AND CHRISTIAN TRADITION

The Scriptures are a great textbook on prayer, especially the psalms and the canticles. They show an intimate picture of the prayer lives of many people. Imagination played an especially important role in the personal prayer of the psalmists. The Twenty-third Psalm is an outstanding example of imaginative prayer.

The next time you have your Bible out, just thumb through the Psalms. Look at how many powerful picture images are painted by the authors. Look at the visualizations that the other biblical writers use in their prayers, such as this powerful image: "The waves of death encompassed me, the torrents of perdition assailed me. . . . In my distress I called upon the Lord; to my God I called. . . . He reached from on high, he took me, he drew me out of many waters" (2 Sam. 22:5, 7, 17).

The Age of Faith, that high point of Christian experience from 1050 to 1350, was a time of wonder, a time of imagination. This age produced the great cathedrals. Christian art, Christian music, all helped the use of the imagination. The great cathedrals such as Chartres and Notre Dame have been called picture Bibles because of their very construction; their window paintings, their vaults of heaven powerfully stimulate the imagination.

The builder of the first Gothic church, Abbot Suger, gives us great insight into the power of imagination and prayer when he describes how he felt on entering the first Gothic church building in 1144. The colored glass construction of the church, he said, had a powerful ability to transform "that which is material to that which is immaterial . . . then it seems to me that I see myself dwelling, as it were, in some strange region of the universe which neither exists entirely in the slime of earth nor entirely in the purity of heaven; and that, by the grace of God, I can be transported from the inferior to that higher world."

So many things that are a part of Christianity today are meant to have the same effect upon our prayer as the visualizations of the Scripture writers and the cathedral builders. The eucharistic service is a drama, an acting out, an imagination. Church buildings, church windows, hymns, full as they are of images, also have this effect. Sadly, we have forgotten how to use our imaginations. We have forgotten the power of the nonrational. As Carl

Jung says, "We are, indeed, the rightful heirs of Christian symbolism, but this inheritance we have somehow squandered."

Guided Prayer Experiences

The prayer experiences or guided meditations in this book may seem to you like a new, modern way of praying. Actually, they are simply modern expressions of very ancient ways of praying. The Twenty-third Psalm puts the listener into a green pasture, carries him through a valley, lets oil stream down his head, and has him picture God as Shepherd. The Hebrews often recited psalms to the stilling, relaxing music of the lyre. The listener was deeply relaxed by the music and soothing words, and filled with healing, spiritual imagery.

The chants of the early church also had a soothing, relaxing quality. The words, either from Scripture or based on Scripture, filled these early Christians with the imagery of their faith. Specific meditations or poems, usually read to the background of soft music, were also composed. One of the greatest composers of such "guided prayer experiences" was St. Paulinus of Nola, a married bishop who lived in the fourth century. Here are a few lines from one of his image-filled poems:

Lighten yourselves in preparation for Christ, and being now relieved of your burdensome luggage, free your feet of its bonds. Become naked in this world to be clothed in abundance of light. . . . May the clouds which transport saints readily bear you in their unsubstantial grasp. . . . And may God steep you in His brightness that the shining glory of eternal life may draw your mortality within it.

St. Bonaventure, the first great Franciscan scholar, wrote guided meditations that were typical of many other authors during the thirteenth century. His work called *The Tree of Life* is essentially a long guided prayer experience that carries the listener or reader into depth prayer through the use of imagery that calls forth all the senses. Here are some brief excerpts that give a taste of what the book is like. Writing of the light of the annunciation, he says: "Oh, if you could feel in some way the quality and intensity of that fire sent from heaven, the refreshing coolness that accompanied it, the consolation it imparted." In the section of the meditation that deals with Jesus' birth, he says: ". . . embrace that divine manger; press your lips upon and kiss the boy's feet. Then in your mind keep the shepherd's watch. . . . Receive the infant in your arms."

Many of the evangelical hymns create much the same type prayer experience. Imagery and music blend to reach the believer's inner core with the power of the gospel. In one such hymn Charles Wesley, the cofounder of the Methodist movement, wrote: "The light of life eternal darts into our souls a dazzling ray, / a drop of heaven overflows our hearts, and deluges the house of clay."

The prayer experiences in this book are inspired by this old tradition of guided Christian imagery. They put that imagery in today's language and forms, but the roots of such prayer experiences are ancient.

5

HOW TO DO IT—IT'S EASIER THAN YOU THINK

The fact that you have read this far indicates that you are interested in learning how to meditate. You sense that new and fresh dimensions of living and loving can open up to you. But you may also be frightened. Whenever we start something new, especially something that involves us as totally as meditation, we fear we will fail.

For most of us, especially the most "successful" of us, our lives have been a series of obstacle courses—school, job-hunting, dating, and so on. Fear of failure has been a constant companion in many of life's endeavors. So as you begin to deepen your prayer you are probably asking, "Is this something else I might fail at?"

I have some shocking and refreshing news for you: it is impossible to try to pray and fail, just as it is impossible to try to love God and fail! Trying to love God is loving him and trying to pray is praying.

Imagine a group of office workers gathered around the coffeepot at break time. They talk about their toddlers, their young children. The smallest action a child takes to show love to parents brings great delight to their hearts. A color drawing given to mother makes her heart leap, no matter that the grass is a purple streak and the sky smudgy yellow. You would never hear one of these office workers say, "My little girl tried to love me with a picture but drew it messy so she failed in loving me." On the contrary, even the slightest, most muddled action of a young child to express love to a parent usually brings joy, just as the first mutters that sound like "Mama" or "Daddy" bring delight.

So it is with God. Our slightest effort as his children to love him in prayer causes his heart to leap. As St. Theophan the Recluse puts it: "Take one feeble step toward God and He will take a thousand toward you."

Trying to pray is praying. You cannot fail! No matter how boring, how dry, how distracted or reluctant your quiet time may be, your prayer, your meditation, reaches beyond the heavens.

When and Where

The first and only commandment in meditation is to relax. This is truly a "let go and let God" type of prayer. We get out of the driver's seat and let him in.

It is usually helpful to wait two hours after a heavy meal and one hour after a substantial snack. It is hard to pray deeply when the body is actively involved in digestion. Also, don't pick your sleepiest time to pray.

The place should be as quiet and as private as possible, but if you have a houseful of children and pets, the Lord understands and will give you grace in any situation.

Begin, either before or after you have relaxed, to talk to God as a friend. Tell him what is going on in you, thank him, and be personal. Give yourself over to him for the period of meditation you are about to begin. Ask him to do with you what he wills. A good prayer of abandonment is simply, "Father, into your hands I commend my spirit."

Don't kneel for meditative prayer. Kneeling at other times is fine, but if you kneel for meditation your mind will be on your aching knees and not on resting in God. Sitting in a chair that is not too hard and not too soft is usually the best position. Keep your spine relatively straight, but not rigid. Lying on the floor, especially on your back, is a great position that keeps the itches and twitches of your body from bothering you. The drawback is that many tend to go to sleep in this position, especially early in the morning. If this is your problem, then this position is not for you.

The Shocking News About Wandering Thoughts

Here you are in your chair; you have given yourself to God in your prayer and started your meditation. Then, after a few minutes, suddenly you realize you have wandered from what you were meditating on. You are thinking about the pizza you are going to have for supper or the spat you just had with a neighbor. Here is where wandering thoughts come in, and here it is that many think they have failed at prayer.

I have some shocking information for you. We all have wandering thoughts in our prayer. I'm fairly certain Jesus did. He was human and human beings have busy "attics." Wandering thoughts, no matter what they are, are to be expected. This haze of thoughts was with us all along, buried deep within us, with a good strong cork stopping up the bottle. It was there unnoticed, causing irritability, high blood pressure, and fatigue. In meditation, you allow God to uncork you and a parade of cloudy images and thoughts marches by.

The reason this takes place is because you are being emptied out. Celano said of St. Francis's prayer times that "he made room for Jesus Christ in the inner recesses of his heart." Letting this stream of thoughts parade by us and then out of us empties us so that there is more room inside for God. The good news is that wandering thoughts don't mean failure; they are part of the process.

Don't try to fight wandering thoughts or you will be like Brer Rabbit fighting the tar baby. The more you fight the more you get stuck in the tar. You gave yourself to God for your prayer time and what happens to you during it is his business. You did not will to have wandering thoughts. It happened to you before you noticed it. Cistercian father William Menninger, in an audiotape on centering prayer, has a fantastic thought on this. He says,

"If in the midst of your thirty-minute prayer time, you stop your prayer a hundred times and have to return to it a hundred times, you have made one hundred separate acts of loving God." When you realize your mind has wandered, gently return to your prayer. Slightly prefer your prayer phrase to your wandering thoughts and images.

"HOLY DROWSINESS"

There is more shocking good news about prayer. Sleepiness doesn't mean failure. Many contemplatives of the tradition speak of the sleep of contemplation. "I sleep but my soul it keeps watch," said St. Bernard of Clairvaux. "Contemplative prayer is a resting, a resting in the arms of our Father. Most of us get sleepy when we rest."

Many of the mystical ascetical theologians speak of sleepiness as a sign of a deepening prayer life. St. Teresa of Ávila called it "holy drowsiness." St. Francis of Sales said, "I had rather be asleep on the breast of God than awake in any other place." This corresponds to what scientists say of meditative states. In meditation prayer you are often in a "theta" state, which is a state of restful alertness. People often feel sleepy in this state.

What if you actually fall asleep in prayer, into the snoring type of sleep? First of all, a good preventive for this is to pray at your most awake times, get plenty of daily exercise, and sleep enough at night. Beyond this, there is not much you can do. You do not will to fall asleep. The last act of your will before you fall asleep is an act of loving God, so you fall asleep in his arms. As the great fourteenth-century work on contemplation, *The Cloud of Unknowing,* says: "If in the midst of this work of love [contemplation] you should fall asleep, praise God." Well put!

USING THE IMAGINATION IN PRAYER

Most of the meditations in this book call for some use of the imagination. When we were little, imagination came easily. We knew the language of imagination before we knew the language of words. But years of sitting six hours a day in hard school desks, usually bored, caused our imaginative abilities to atrophy.

The first step to using the imagination in your prayer time is to relax. Relaxation releases the ability to imagine. Exercises and suggestions in the following chapter can help you learn to relax.

Second, remember that we experience the imagination in different ways. Imagination is more than just seeing with the mind's eye. It involves all the senses—taste, touch, hearing, smell, the sense of body movement. Some people are better at imagining certain senses than other senses. Some people rarely "see" or experience anything. Rather, they have a "sense" of the scene imagined without visualizing, hearing, or touching. Having this sense of the scene to be imagined is just as powerful as having 3-D Technicolor imagination. My own way of imagination is a mixture of "sensing" and seeing. I get only fleeting glimpses of the scene to be imagined, but I have a real sense of being there.

Finally, whatever your experience of imagination, learn to be at home with it. The more you actively practice imagination, the more acute your imagination will become. Like television sets that are picking up a distant station, we all have static and other bleeding in across the scene. A relaxed attitude about your imagination, whatever your experience, is the key to unlocking it. Remember, if you try, you can't fail. Even the slightest glimpse or sense of the scene to be imagined integrates us, opens us to God, and helps us to become whole.

How to Use the Prayer Experiences in This Book

The prayer experiences in this book are designed to guide you gently into depth prayer. Some you will take to immediately; others you may discover are not right for you now. You might return to them later and find that they take on a new life. Some will be special and you will return to them often and probably have a different experience each time. All of them, it is hoped, will help you learn to design and pray meditations that are uniquely your own.

Read over the special prayer experiences once or twice slowly. Then close your eyes, go through a period of relaxation, and carry yourself through the experience. Don't worry about getting everything exactly right.

Another way of using the prayer experiences is to gently, softly, and with many pauses, record them on cassette and play them back to yourself.

Another variation is to use them with one or more friends. You can take turns guiding one another through the prayer experiences by slowly reading them aloud. This can be a great way to strengthen and build spiritual friendships.

Certain instrumental music deeply relaxes you and unlocks the imagination. Classical pieces, especially certain baroque compositions, have this ability. The last five years have also seen new music designed especially to deepen relaxation and meditation as well as release imaginative ability. You might want to try playing such music as background to your meditation.

6

RELAXATION—SINKING INTO GRACE

Anxiety, worry, insomnia, irritability, heartburn, indigestion, headaches, high blood pressure—these and similar maladies are symptoms of a stressful existence. And how little most of us know about ways to relieve stress.

A bird sits on a tree branch. A cat curls up in the sunlit spot by a window. A dog lies on the grass, head between its paws. Animals know how to relax, naturally. But we busy human beings have forgotten how to relax—and it's killing us.

Relaxation revitalizes us, renews us, gives us time to rejuvenate both physically and emotionally. In Christian relaxation our being lets go in God's love. As the seventeenth-century Lutheran pastor Jakob Böhme said, "We sink into the ground of His mercy. . . . His love is there and leads you from anxiety into God."

Relaxation is essential for imagination prayer. As Adelaide Bry and Marjorie Bair put it, "Letting go into relaxation is like dimming the lights in a movie theater. Both let you see the images on the screen."

Much of our tension is held in our muscles. Relaxing the muscles helps us let go of tension.

The following technique is helpful in relaxing. Read it over several times, slowly; then close your eyes and repeat the main ideas to yourself. You will quietly be telling the different parts of your body to relax. You will be amazed at the results.

RELAXATION EXERCISE

Take time to center, be still. Allow the stillness to sweep over you.

In your imagination, Jesus comes up to you. He sets up a little table right in front of you and on that table he puts a box with the lid open. You know that he wants you to put your pain into that box. Allow yourself to become aware of whatever tension you feel, whatever heartache. As you become aware, reach with your hand to your stomach or chest area as though you were pulling out the inward pain. Now put it into the box. See how very light you feel as you pull out the tension. When you have finished, close the box. Jesus takes the box, opens it near the heart area of his chest, and absorbs the pain into himself.

Now Jesus puts a bucket of water on the table and instantly you know what this is. This is the water of everlasting life that Jesus said would well up within us into eternal life. Swirl your hands in the water. Notice how very special that water feels. Your hand, as you swirl it, begins to tingle; currents of warmth pass through it. As you swirl your hand in the warming, soothing water, the radiant love, the tingling, refreshing feeling passes up through your arm to your heart. Now touch your hand to any part of your body that is feeling the ache of tension and let the healing, tingling glow pass from your hand to that area. Feel the tension dissolve away. Put your hand back in and swirl it and repeat this until you have touched different areas of your body in need of relaxation.

Our painful emotions are held in part by the involuntary tensing of our muscles. Put your hand on any muscles that are tight with tension. Become aware of where you sense emotional pain in your different muscles, perhaps also in your heart area or your stomach area. Swirl your hand in the refreshing water and let the tingling, healing feeling in your hand pass to your heart area, if that is where the emotional pain is, or to your stomach area, your back, or your head—wherever the emotional pain is manifesting itself. Repeat this as often as you would like.

CENTERING PRAYER—A WAY OF RELAXATION

Centering prayer is an ancient and deeply stilling form of Christian prayer. Find a short prayer that is meaningful to you such as "Abba, Father," "Lord Jesus, have mercy," "Lord Jesus, Healer, heal me," or some other prayful phrase. Repeat the phrase silently. If you are distracted, gently return to your prayer phrase.

You will be surprised by how a few minutes of this prayer calms you and revitalizes you.

PART TWO

Experiencing God's Love

7

A LOVE THAT CHANGES US

Time and time again, I see the change that takes place when people discover the love of God made visible in Jesus.

My friend Billy's experience beautifully illustrates this. Billy is an ex-army officer in his early forties, an avid jogger and veteran of the Boston Marathon. He discovered meditation before he discovered Christ.

I met him with a glass of fruit punch in his hand at the home of mutual friends during a New Year's Eve party. My friends introduced us saying, "I know you two will have a lot in common. You're both interested in meditation." Meeting someone with such a similar interest, I became my overtalkative, excited self. I went on and on about Paul's understanding of love, the writings of Teresa of Ávila, John and Charles Wesley. But I noticed something wasn't connecting. Billy's eyes kept moving up and down in little jerks. I knew it was time to shut up and let him speak.

After he had talked a few minutes, I knew his experience of meditation was different from mine. Billy had been searching for inner pathways but had avoided Christian pathways. The preceding few years had taken him on quite a journey. Many of the things he looked into were beneficial and valid in themselves. He had visited American Indian communities in the Southwest and talked to their spiritual masters. He had read meditation manuals and was in the midst of working on a graduate degree in counseling psychology. He had experienced many techniques from Eastern religions. Yet, I sensed it was not all coming together for him. There seemed to be little integration; things were not connecting.

Billy talked about the awesome power he believed our minds have to control our outer environment. It appeared that meditation for him was a set of methods he could use to control both his internal world and the very concrete world around him.

I didn't see Billy again for a year. During that interval he passed through stormy times. He and his wife separated. He changed jobs. He experienced his limits as a person. His techniques were not enough. He knew he was no longer in control of either his inside world or his outside world. And he came in touch with the limitless love of God in Christ in Christianity. He made a decision to be baptized, confirmed, and received into the church.

When he came to see us at our house just after that decision, this strong man broke down and shook with sobs. Accepting his limits, willing to give up control was not easy. Then it seemed day by day a change took place in him. Meditation, rather than being a means of control, now became a means of experiencing God's accepting love. An amazing personal integration, a new tenderness came to his personality. He began to form many close Christian friendships.

A year after his baptism Billy took over leadership of the parish youth group. It flourished. Many of his natural abilities blossomed. His problems didn't magically work themselves out; not everything he has done has been blessed with the Midas touch of success. But his walk, the look in his eyes, the gentleness of his voice tell of a deep ability to love himself that has come through accepting God's acceptance.

INCARNATE LOVE MEANS EVERYDAY LOVE

God is boundless love, an eternity of caring. "God is love, and he who abides in love abides in God" (1 John 4:16).

But the statement "God is love" by itself is not enough. The consumer society that surrounds us too greatly influences our concept of love. This popular view of love is as sticky sweet, as unstable and mushy as tapioca pudding. Popular songs pound in the idea that love is being hooked on feelings. For the statement "God is love" to catch our attention and change us, it must be fleshed out, become everyday, approachable, incarnate.

And this is exactly what happened in Jesus. In him the endless ocean of love that is God became touchable, approachable, real. Infinite, ineffable love became an everyday love. From his earliest days, Jesus experienced a mysterious love all around him and in the center of his being. At some point, in the most natural way, he began to call this love "Abba," the Aramaic word for *Daddy*. This was the image that most fully expressed his relationship to that love. Later, he came to know that the love he called "Daddy" was also his own innermost identity. Through the earthy, concrete stories he told, and through the story that was his life, he made that love real for us.

Jesus turned the world's understanding of things upside down. His Father loved with a scandalous love—prostitutes, drunkards, tax collectors were special objects of his passionate caring. He was the shepherd who would leave the ninety-nine sheep for the one lost sheep; the father who embraced and kissed the returning son who had squandered all that the father had given him. He was the woman (yes, Jesus did compare God to a woman) who swept the house clean searching for the lost coin. Jesus himself showed that searching love of God by mingling with prostitutes and drunkards, and even having people hurl at him the accusation of being a glutton and drunkard. By the way Jesus lived his life, he showed what God was like, reaching to people in the deepest level of their woundedness, loving the undeserving.

In the gospel of John, Jesus unsettles his disciples' view of the order of things by becoming their servant—washing their feet. On the cross, his ultimate giving of himself, he shows the depths to which God goes to win us back and to heal our wounded hearts and our wounded world. And through his resurrection he promises a future in which this loving God will win out, will have the final say over the forces of dehumanization, destruction, and fear that are part of our lives and part of the life of our world.

The stories Jesus told and the story of his life are full of earthy, ordinary details of everyday life—details of business, finances, farming, sickness, death. God's love can come to us in this ordinary, everyday world in which we live our lives.

When I am filled with self-doubt, when some of my projects have failed, when my stomach aches with disappointment, I need a God who loves me despite my seeming failure. I need a God who sees right past the layers of falsity and fear in my personality to the wonderful, unique creature that is the real me. This experience of the mystery of his love helps me believe in myself again. And when I have hurt others, hurt God, and hurt myself by running off my own way, he receives me back, kisses and embraces me, like the father who embraced the prodigal son.

I need the experience of this love every day in the little concrete events of my life. From spats I have with friends to frustrations over finances, he greets me with the good news that I am loved, accepted—and his love speeds me along my journey to wholeness.

His love is there to challenge me each time I decide to receive it. I know that it's risky business, because when I open my heart, my being, my everyday life to the God who loves like the God who reveals himself through Jesus, I have no other choice but to struggle to love like that. Each time I open myself up to that love, that love prods me on, challenges me to begin, even in some small measure, to love in the same way. I know that if I open myself to his love, I open myself to change. When I let him hold me close I find that he needs me as much as I need him, and this scares me. He needs me to be an agent of his peace, to weep with those who weep, to greet him in "the least of those my brothers."

BARRIERS TO EXPERIENCING GOD'S LOVE

The daily images that bombard us—at work, at school, and on television—do not reinforce the idea that we are the children of a loving Father who holds us tenderly in the palms of his hands. So if we wish to experience God's love, we need to expose ourselves daily to the reality of that love and the reality of our daily need for that love. Christian prayer, meditation, the eucharist, Scripture reflection, loving connections with other Christians are all pathways we can open daily, pathways for the sunlight of God's love to reach the cellars of our being.

Another barrier is when we conceive of the experience of God only as an emotion. We think we're experiencing God's love only when we "feel" it. Yes, there will be times when our emotions vibrate like violin strings from the touch of his hand upon us. Such times should be graciously received for they are mountaintop experiences that help us see the whole of our lives. But a life that moved from just one high to another would be an artificial life, an unreal life. We can experience his love even when we don't feel it, even if our feelings are as dry as the sands of the desert.

Marriage shows this clearly. How many times I have seen people transformed after they marry, especially when there is a strong, loving marriage with open communication. One friend married several months ago for the first time. A new mellowness rooted itself in his personality. Overly masculine and controlled before, he began to approach life with a feminine tenderness along with his natural masculine strength. A source of fresh life welled up in him. The daily experience of someone special loving him, spending his time at home with someone who cherished him instead of by himself, all had a steadying, healing, transforming effect on his personality. Yes, there were high and giddy times for him that showed in the brightness of his eyes. He also had his low moments and his in-between moments. Whatever his feelings, every week of his marriage, so it seems, has increased his ability to cherish and care about others. An increasing capacity to experience creation around him blossomed.

So it is with God. His love is no constant high. Rather, we open ourselves to the presence of One who steadily loves us. We flower, we look upon the world with a loving gaze. Compassion takes root deep within us. Through painful times and joyous times, we travel the journey of our lives with the deepening knowledge that we are steadied by the Eternal Lover beside us.

There will be times too of wandering the desert—times of dryness when God seems far away, times of seeming lostness when his love does not move us. As we grow in faith, though, we will find that these times of feeling lost are our greatest homecoming. At such times, knowing that we cannot heal ourselves, we find out that we need the help of Another. Only the taste of redemption, the touch of salvation, the ways of an overpowering grace can restore to us the precious gift of our humanity. It is the love of Another from outside us who calls with strength and tenderness, but One who is also hidden intimately in the secret recesses, the inner chambers of our souls. Then we know that we need a Savior, that we need redemption, that we need wave after wave of grace.

It is at such a time that we know ourselves to be like Peter, who sank as he tried to walk on water—only the touch of Christ's hand could save him.

The Purpose of the Following Meditations

The following meditations are to help us open our personalities even more to the experience of God's love. All prayer does this—any type of prayer. The meditations in this section and in the section that follows are especially designed to highlight our awareness that we stand in the presence of One who loves us. They bombard us with images and affirmations that help us open the cellar doors within us. These meditations are designed to help us allow the love of the Eternal Lover to meet us in the stuff of daily living.

8

THIS IS ME, LORD, RIGHT NOW

One of the main reasons that prayer can feel artificial is that we often hide our real feelings from ourselves and from God. As T. S. Eliot put it, "We prepare a face to meet the faces that we meet."

Hiding from others, God, and ourselves absorbs a great deal of emotional and physical energy and leaves us strained and tired. When we take time to notice and acknowledge our emotions, or how our body feels at the moment—when we are honest—the energy we tie up in repression can be redirected for more effective living and loving. Our whole being loosens up and relaxes. We are freed to be more present to the here and now. So many of the authors of Scripture had that honest awareness of themselves. When we acknowledge where we are at the moment, it's easier for God's love to penetrate us more deeply.

Noticing our feelings is different from being overwhelmed by them. It is one thing to fly into an uncontrolled rage and strike out at a friend or family member and quite another to prayerfully acknowledge our emotions and say to ourselves and to God: "I'm feeling intense anger right now."

Roberto Assagioli, a psychotherapist and author who incorporates many ideas from Christian spiritual masters in his writings, says: "We are dominated by everything with which our self becomes identified. We can dominate and control everything from which we disidentify ourselves." Frances E. Vaughan, in her book called *Awakening Intuition*, beautifully describes this process: "Thus you may be aware of having fear, for example, as part of the contents of consciousness, without becoming identified with it or controlled by it. Unlike repressed feelings, which distort perception, contribute to chronic tension, and distract one's attention from the present, emotions which are observed . . . come and go and change naturally."

PRAYER EXPERIENCE

Take time to relax and be still. Let your attention move over your body. Notice any tense or tight muscles. Notice any physical pain or discomfort. Become aware of the emotions you are feeling now. Feel them. What fears are you feeling? What guilts? What anger? What joys are you feeling? What feelings of affection?

What are some of the thoughts you are thinking? Don't judge or try to change what you are feeling or thinking. Just notice and acknowledge.

When you have noticed where you are right now, give yourself as you are, where you are, to God.

Pray this prayer or a similar prayer of your own:

"Here I am Lord. This is me right now. I place myself as I am before your all-caring and all-forgiving love. I open myself to your healing touch. I open myself to the unfathomable mystery of your love. I allow you to love me."

Rest in silence several minutes in the sunlight of his love. Pause in silence before God's love.

SCRIPTURE JOURNEY

And in that region there were shepherds out in the field, keeping watch over their flock by night. And an angel of the Lord appeared to them, and the glory of the Lord shone around them, and they were filled with fear. And the angel said to them, "Be not afraid; for behold, I bring you good news of a great joy which will come to all the people; for to you is born this day in the city of David a Savior, who is Christ the Lord. And this will be a sign for you: you will find a babe wrapped in swaddling cloths and lying in a manger." And suddenly there was with the angel a multitude of the heavenly host praising God and saying,

"Glory to God in the highest,
and on earth peace among men
with whom he is pleased!''

When the angels went away from them into heaven, the shepherds said
to one another, "Let us go over to Bethlehem and see this thing that has
happened, which the Lord has made known to us." And they went with
haste, and found Mary and Joseph, and the babe lying in a manger.

(LUKE 2:8–16)

Just as you are now, go to the scene in Bethlehem. It's okay if
the scene in your mind's eye looks like a Christmas postcard. Go
there and look at the child. What do you see in his eyes? Is he
playful? Take him in your arms. Feel the tenderness from inside
yourself, the warm melting tenderness the infant calls forth. What
are you feeling? What are you thinking?

Now look at the infant Jesus for a while and drink in the radiance
of the moment. One reason that we feel so safe and so secure
around infants, one reason they bring out such a giddy spontaneity,
a radiant glow inside us, is that they need us. They need us to love
them; they need us to share their wonder at the world. You can be
yourself around an infant; there is no need to pretend. That's what
God was doing. God not only came down here to die for us, to
suffer for us, to redeem us. He also comes to us in the form of a
vulnerable child, a child who needs our love—and we all need to
be needed. We need to be needed for just who we are.

Nothing makes a roomful of people come alive like the presence
of an infant. When a group of adults are around an infant, it is as
though they have permission to be silly again, permission to be
childlike themselves, to be amazed at the world as an infant is
amazed. It is as though in being around an infant, we can enter into
that time that was once ours, when the world and each moment
in it were fresh and new. We feel safe around infants; we know they
will not judge us. Few things draw out our trust like a vulnerable
infant. We can be ourselves, we can let the light and happy side
of us come forth, and we are able to be energized afresh by God.

That's what happened to the shepherds in this story. They were not planning to meet the Messiah that evening. They were not preparing themselves for anything; they were just being themselves, doing what shepherds do, intently involved with their work. So they were astonished by the angels, amazed by the infant.

9

THE GENTLE STRENGTH OF REMEMBERING

How often my mind and heart return to my grandparents' one-bedroom cotton-mill house. I have learned as much about prayer and meditation from simple-hearted people like them as from the scores of books on spirituality I have studied.

Brought up in the rough days following the Civil War by her dirt-poor grandmother, my own grandmother as a child knew the daily threat to survival that people in Bangladesh and Calcutta live with today. She and her family would go for weeks with nothing to subsist on but moldy cornmeal and milk from an old cow. Illness, possible death of family members, and the threat of starvation constantly walked beside them. Those rough times made my grandmother strong, sweet, and steady rather than bitter. Their struggle knitted her and her family closer to one another and to God.

After she married, she and my Cherokee grandfather held stable mill jobs during hard times. The dinner table was usually filled with down-and-out relatives and acquaintances. A black family with several small children and no jobs or income took their meals with my grandparents.

My grandmother didn't learn to read until after she had given birth to three children; but there was a wisdom and compassion in her bright eyes that gave evidence of a knowledge far deeper than could ever be contained in libraries. During the times I spent with her as a child she would often get out the bulky white family Bible, sit in the rocker by the corner, and slowly read each word. Her eyes would be half-closed and she would just drift off.

I knew what she was doing; she was remembering—remembering the closeness and warmth of her early days, all the people she had known; remembering the times that God had touched her in the midst of crisis; remembering those who had died.

As she went about her housework, the radio stayed on the country channel. From time to time they played the sentiment-filled gospel song, "Precious Memories." "Precious memories, how they linger, how they satisfy my soul . . . in the stillness of the twilight, precious sacred scenes unfold." Her eyes would become moist and she would lean on her broom, or take the iron off the clothes and set it upright for a moment, and drift. Her facial muscles would relax and an aura of peace and strength would envelop her. These times of going back to the strengths of the past were much of the source of the beauty in my grandmother.

Many ways of praying are so obvious that we miss them. Remembering can lead to the deepest meditative states. When we remember the special times God has blessed us, that strength becomes present to us in the here and now. We also widen our capacity to experience God's love and caring in the present.

Remembering relaxes us. The famous Brazilian soccer player Pelé often prepared for games by remembering, remembering times from his childhood when he played soccer barefoot along Brazilian beaches, or some of his best experiences of winning. For especially difficult games he would take up to thirty minutes of remembering.

The Scriptures frequently speak of remembering. The psalmists remember the goodness of God; they remember his mercy. "I remember the days of old; I meditate on all that you have done; I muse on what your hands have wrought. . . . Let me hear . . . of your steadfast love, for in you I put my trust" (Ps. 143:5–8). So much of the prayer of the psalmists was simply remembering. The Hebrew word for remembering is *zicar;* it means remembering in such a strong way that the past becomes present.

PRAYER EXPERIENCE

Find a comfortable place. Relax. Take some time for the ease of centering prayer. Gently let your mind float back to times you especially felt God's loving presence. Perhaps it was a walk at night when all the stars were out. Perhaps it was your first communion, or a prayer time, or a retreat—a time when you felt God's love coming to you through another person, a time of crisis in which you felt an unexpected comfort. Perhaps it was listening to special music. Remember the sights, the tastes, the sounds, the feelings. Feel the feelings again. Relive the experience. This is a way of praying, a prayer script you can return to many times and call forth many strengthening memories from the past to help you live more fully in the present and the future.

SCRIPTURE JOURNEY

Therefore, since we are surrounded by so great a cloud of witnesses, let us also lay aside every weight, and sin which clings so closely, and let us run with perseverance the race that is set before us, looking to Jesus the pioneer and perfecter of our faith, who for the joy that was set before him, endured the cross, despising the shame, and is seated at the right hand of the throne of God. Consider him endured from sinners such hostility against himself, so that you may not grow weary or faint hearted.

(HEB. 12:1–3)

Read the passage above and also read all of Hebrews 11 before you enter into this experience. This particular passage comes after the author of Hebrews has taken the whole eleventh chapter to remember the mighty acts of God among the people of Israel, the deliverance from Egypt, and Abraham's call to faith. In this twelfth chapter, he calls us to remember Jesus, the pioneer and perfecter of our faith.

Each of us has his or her own story of salvation. But we also have the memory of Israel, the memory of the Church.

Close your eyes and take time to recall some of the mighty acts of God in the history of Israel and Jesus. Picture those scenes that come to you easily, perhaps scenes from stained glass windows, perhaps pictures from your Bible or scenes from religious movies, but remember those cords of great deliverance that weave their way throughout the Old Testament, the story of Jesus, and the stories of the early church. Let scenes from Jesus' life pass before you; remember as though you were there. And when you are finished with this remembering, say a prayer of thanksgiving.

10

BEGINNINGS

I was a child who was wanted, longed for, yearned for. The doctors had told my parents that it would be nearly impossible for them to have children. They suffered through twelve years of praying and hoping against hope that they would have a child. So there was great rejoicing when I was born. When I was little, I don't know that it was possible for any child to be loved more than I was loved. My parents have a capacity for tenderness that is unique. I know that that immersion in love has been one of the reasons I search so hard for the love of God in depth prayer, in meditative prayer.

Another major reason is my grandfather, my father's father. I called him Pop. Pop's mother, born and reared in the North Carolina mountains, had been a full-blooded Cherokee. Pop was steeped in an Appalachian wisdom, Cherokee wisdom. He never learned to read or write, yet he was one of the wisest men I have ever known. I learned more from him about silence and contemplation, about harmony with nature, about deep peacefulness than I have from the hundreds of books on theology and spirituality that I have read.

Two pictures dominated the tiny living room of my grandparents' house—the picture I have already mentioned of Jesus standing at the door asking to be let in, and a picture of Jesus at the Last Supper. My cousin Betty, a generation older than I, says that Jesus was very important to Pop. He gave his heart to Jesus in a Baptist church when he was a young man, and he often asked Betty to read to him from the Bible.

There was a strength about Pop, a deep-down, rock-solid

strength. How comfortable he felt with silence and quiet, sitting for long periods in his chair, entering into a rich, alive stillness that showed itself in his face, his heart, his whole being.

Because I was interested in the old times, I asked Pop many questions and delighted in his stories. His face would brighten as I sat there on his footstool, looking at him and he at me. He would tell me things that came from far within himself.

He would tell me marvelous stories of growing up in the mountains of North Carolina, stories of our people that had been handed on to him, stories and parables about animals. I remember just bits and pieces of those stories now. What I mostly remember are the feelings, strong powerful feelings of a different world that I was caught up in when I listened to him. It was as though a whole new reality would spin around us as he spoke—a reality full of peace and delight in the world, in life, in God's creatures; a reality that was at peace with a world in which God was near, not just in the Bible, but shining and reflecting himself to us through all the things around us.

I remember the first night I ever spent apart from my parents; I must have been no more than four or five years old. My father was running a high fever and had to go to the hospital, so my mother went with him. I was restless and worried and twitched about in bed all night, crying lots of little-boy tears. When a nearby neighbor's rooster crowed, I was still awake. With the first hint of dawn, Pop got me up, helped me put on my clothes, and walked with me across the street to a path along the Chattahoochee river. We looked at Grandmother Sun as she came across the horizon above us and then we turned and looked down at the river. We Cherokees personify nature just as Psalm 148 personified nature: "Praise him, sun and moon, praise him, all you shining stars (Ps. 148:3). We call the sun "Grandmother."

There was an interchange of stillness between Pop's heart and the water below and the rising sun. It was as if he were drawing on a deep quiet from creation, a quiet in which God came to us, showing his tender love through the things he made. Then Pop looked at me and gently taught me a Cherokee prayer, a prayer to Grandmother Sun. It goes like this:

> Good morning, Grandmother Sun,
> Good morning, Grandmother,
> I stand in the middle of your sun rays,
> I stand in the middle of your sun rays,
> And by the Creator, I am blessed.

As he said the prayer, I felt some of that stillness.

Part of the pain as I grew up was that nobody else really understood the world quite like Pop. That part of me that tasted the stillness and the wonder and drank in his stories was a part no one else understood. Through Pop, I was being called to a place inside where all things are one. I had known great tenderness from my parents and aunts and uncles and such richness from Pop. But the world of school and the world of my peers laughed at Pop's way of looking at things. So I had to learn to hide that part of me.

To survive I had to push those memories down deep within me. Occasionally Pop would speak some Cherokee to me when no one else was around, probably words he hadn't spoken since he was my age. I'm the only one who remembers Pop doing this. I'm sure many of the things he shared with me were things only partially remembered from when he was little.

Pop was his full-blooded Indian mother's first child. She was a "healer," a "granny woman." My dad said she could cure anything with herbs. And, in part because of his experiences of her, my own father developed the heart of a healer, the heart of a peacemaker.

Pop seemed always to be going back to the pantry. I used to delight in Pop's trips to that wondrously mysterious place. There were all sorts of bright and interesting things there. It seemed that almost every week he would bring me an old silver dollar from the pantry. Some had dates that went back to the 1880s. He would also show me things he said he would give me when I grew up: a mold that you poured lead into to make a bullet; an old iron, black and rusted with age, the type they used, he said, long before he was born. There were all sorts of things buried in the deep darkness of that pantry.

One day, a day I will always remember, I was sitting on his footstool and he in his chair, and he said, "Let's go to the pantry." I followed him with delight and expectation; I saw him pull up a board and under that board was a wampum—a sacred wampum, a white beaded belt that Cherokees hold when they say prophetic or very important things. I don't know if it was made of shells or beads, but it had yellowed and looked very old. Pop had me sit in his chair, and he sat on the stool. I didn't understand what was going on, but I wasn't afraid. He wrapped the wampum around our hands clasped together, and he began to sing quietly some chants in Cherokee. I could just catch a word here and there, but it was as though powerful streams of warmth flowed from his hands through my arms and into my heart as he chanted. I sat there crying—not my little-boy tears but tears such as I saw women cry when people came down to accept Christ at the invitation at the Baptist church. I saw that Pop was crying too. I had never seen Pop cry before and I never would again, nor do I know anyone else who ever saw him cry.

I didn't know what all that meant. But I knew it was sacred and special and I knew that he was passing on to me something rich and deep within him from our Cherokee people, something that had been passed to him by his full-blooded mother, a way of looking at things.

Pop became seriously ill with cancer and fought a long fight that lasted five years. He was never fully himself again. Things changed and I didn't have a chance to spend much time alone with him again. I gradually began to stuff the things he had taught me into some hidden corner within. Nobody at school talked like that or saw the world like that. None of my friends and acquaintances seemed to understand when I told them about those things. People just didn't see the world that way.

Two or three months before Pop died, my junior high school went on half-day rotation and I spent my afternoons off with him and Granny. One day, when he looked particularly ill, he said something Indian again. As he looked at me, his eyes cleared for a moment and he smiled and said, "You walk in my soul." That was the Cherokee way of saying, "I love you." Then he said, "Remember, I used to live in Leicester, North Carolina. I want you to go there and see it someday." It was twenty years later but one day I did.

I stuffed those things so far down that barely a trace of them remained in my conscious mind. I turned numb before Pop died, so very numb. I didn't cry at his funeral. I just didn't feel anything. The numbness didn't take away the pain of losing him; it just buried it deep within.

In the years after Pop's death much of my sensitivity to emotion, to life, shut down. I was a little boy and my loss was overwhelming. I did what many children do at such a time: I hid my memories of Pop deep inside me, walled away from my awareness. It was many years later when I was well along the road to healing, at a time when I was strong enough and secure enough to feel the feelings of loss, that my memories of Pop came back to me.

Robert Herrmann and I were giving a series of retreats and evenings of renewal for the diocese of Marquette in Upper Peninsula Michigan. Our host took us to meet Fr. John Haskell, pastor of the Catholic church on the small Ojibway reservation. Fr. John is an Indian priest of mixed Cherokee and Ojibway heritage. He was both medicine man and Catholic priest to his people, richly blending Indian cultural ways with Christianity. Unity with nature; reverence for life; seeing Gitche Manitou, the Great Spirit, in all things; a communal, noncompetitive approach to life—all these gifts that came to him from his Indian heritage—richly seasoned his Christianity. He viewed life as Pop had viewed it.

As I listened to Fr. John talk I was a bit skeptical of why

anyone would bother with such quaint irrelevant traditions. I briefly mentioned that I was part Indian. I had always known that I was Indian and that as I child I had spent time with Pop, but I held little conscious memory of him. I knew that as a child I had known all the old stories of the Cherokee, but I had no memory of Pop telling them to me. I didn't even think it odd that I had no memories of my grandfather.

When I returned to Georgia I followed up on my talk with Fr. John. I started asking my father questions. He took me to Alabama to see Aunt Nellie, Pop's ninety-year-old sister-in-law. Nellie knew so much and treasured so much.

Something was stirring inside me, something powerful at my very core. Meeting Fr. Haskell had lit a fuse tied to explosive emotions within me. The fuse was slowly burning shorter and shorter.

Not long after visiting with Nellie, I was recounting the conversation with Robert and Pat, my coworkers. A little while after I started talking my eyes burned with tears and an utterly unexpected volcano of emotions burst forth from me in racking, uncontrollable sobs. Robert and Pat sat there with me, warmly present and silent as the pain erupted.

I had finally begun to grieve for Pop. I was finally strong enough to feel the loss, secure enough to at last remember. After the weeping, memories came—a few at first, then more. My grieving is still going on but with it comes the lost joy, the lost wonder. Right along with the hurting comes the mystical gift of my Indian heritage that Pop passed on to me. With it comes the memory of Pop's closeness to Jesus. I have experienced a flood of richness from my time of beginning as a human being—not only memories of Pop but of the wonder-filled early times with my parents, my aunts, my uncles; the knowledge of how deeply and how thoroughly I was loved.

We all have rich resources and memories from our beginnings; we all have the bright heritage from that wondrous fresh world that once was ours. And we all have grieving to do, pain to feel, tears to shed, and people to forgive from those beginning times.

Our relationships with our parents and other close relatives go to the very heart of our own identities. We may hold inside us an unresolved resentment, anger, or deep hurt that we have never opened up for healing. Such buried anger or bitterness impairs our lives in the here and now. We also have bright glowing memories of our parents and close relatives that are hidden away inside. We cannot be selective in our memory. If we exile our hurtful memories, we have to hide away the joyful memories. We have to deny wonder and that whole rich symphony of feelings God made us feel. When we embrace the hurt, then the joy can flood us. When we remember the good memories, we then have the strength and sense of safety we need to face the painful ones. There are strong, wonderful, and powerful gifts from our parents and other close relatives that have gone to sleep inside us; reawakening those can bring a springtime of fresh newness for us.

PRAYER EXPERIENCE

PART I

In this meditation, you are going to go back to the time your mother first held you in her arms. You don't need to know the actual details, but if you do know them that's helpful.

Take time to center, to be still. You may want to use one of the other meditations in this book that is particularly comforting to you. Take time to recall an occasion when your body and your heart vibrated with well-being, when health and energy, joy and happiness welled up within you, when you were surrounded by the radiant light of God's love. Remember such a time for a moment as part of your preparation for this meditation.

You are going to go back to the time of your infancy. Go back to the hospital (or home) where you were born. Your mother is in bed. She looks tired from having given birth. Perhaps she is groggy from the anesthesia. You hear steps. Someone is bringing a baby, the infant you once were. That person gently carries the baby into the room and puts it in your mother's arms. Look at your mother's facial expressions. How does she react? How does the baby respond to the mother? The adult you is in the room watching your mother with the infant. If you sense pain or distress in the room, gently pray in your own way that the healing light of Christ will fill the room to soothe and heal. If there is great rejoicing there, let yourself enter into that. As you are present there, allow the radiant love of the healing Christ to fill the inner spaces of the room.

You say a prayer for the baby and for the mother. In your own words, pray that any hidden pain will come to the surface and be healed. Now the adult you steps over to your mother. You take the baby, the infant you, from her arms. You cradle the baby. See if you can sense the needs of the infant. Pass on to the child your own deep love with the gentleness and tenderness of your touch.

Beside you comes Another. Jesus is there with you. Feel his hand on your shoulder. Feel his robe touch you. Through his touch, he passes on to you the warm compassion of his heart, the graceful and gentle power that heals. Your breathing becomes easy and slow as you are filled with a heavenly calm, and you pass that tenderness on to the infant.

PART II

Take time to be still, to be centered, to recall the Lord's love. When you have entered into that place of restful quiet, go back to your room in your parents' home when you were a child. Look at the different things in the room. Smell the smells. What do you feel now? Happiness? Sadness? Homesickness? Let yourself be aware of your feelings. Don't try to judge, just acknowledge.

Now someone comes into the room—your mother. She sits down and you take a seat facing her. What do you feel as you see her? Just feel, don't judge.

Your mother says to you, "Is there something you would like

to tell me that you've never really told me before?'' Somehow as you hear her, you know that she means it, that this time no matter what you say she will listen. Now say to her what you'd like to tell her. How does she respond to your words? She asks you a question and you know that she really wants to know. She asks, ''Is there some way that I could have loved you better?'' Pause a moment and tell her. It feels safe to tell her because you know this time she really wants to know. You answer her. If hurt emerges within, in your imagination, tell her you forgive her for ways she may have hurt you. Do this only when you feel ready. If you feel ready, embrace her. Linger awhile in the embrace, experiencing for a time the warm glow of the embrace.

Now you ask her, ''Is there some way I could have loved you better?'' And gently and calmly she tells you. How do you respond to what she says? You ask her if there is something she would like to tell you. And she does. How does it feel when you hear that?

If your mother is still alive, ask her, ''Is there some important way I can love you better now?'' and hear what she has to say.

She embraces you and tells you she forgives you. Trust in that embrace. A third joins you. It is Jesus, putting one arm on each of you, joining in your embrace. A shimmering stillness, a quiet rest comes over you as Jesus touches you both.

Repeat this prayer experience with your father or other close relative from your childhood.

11

THE HEALING THERAPY OF GOD'S FORGIVENESS

So many people whom God uses as special instruments of his Presence speak constantly of how much they have been forgiven. They remember and cherish God's forgiveness. Like the prostitute who anointed Jesus' feet, they are forgiven much because they love much (Luke 7:47).

St. Francis of Assisi experienced the healing therapy of forgiveness and awoke to a world fresh with wonder. This playboy turned into a joyful troubadour of God's love. He and the community around him changed their world.

In his prayer and in his conversation Francis frequently recalled how God's mercy overwhelmed him and redirected him. One day as Francis and his big burly companion Masseo walked barefooted on a dusty Italian road, Masseo turned to him and said, "Francis, why you? Why is the whole world following after you? Let's face it, Francis, you're not a very handsome person. You're not much to look at. You're not very educated; you don't even know much Latin. Why you, Francis? Why is the whole world following after you?"

Francis paused a moment, turned his eyes to Masseo, and said, "It's like this, Masseo, the Most High looked down from heaven and he couldn't find anyone more foolish or full of folly, more inadequate, and he had mercy on me; and expressed his love to me. That's so it could clearly be seen, Masseo, that what good I do is of the Most High and not of me."

An attitude like Francis's can make us mirrors that reflect God's love. It's the realization that we are what we are because of God's constant forgiveness. Through such brokenness, through such earthen vessels God's love flows.

The reality of sin is ever before each of us. Sin comes from putting ourselves first. When I center on myself to the exclusion of God and others, I build barriers between myself and God, between myself and those around me. If I hurt and use others, I hurt and use God. Selfish centering on myself is sin. It is deadening and brings death.

To live in today's world and not talk about sin is to live in a constant state of denial, in an unreal world. God says an incredible yes to us, a profound yes, a yes that affirms all creation, affirms our essential goodness, and celebrates us as persons.

If we are true to Scripture, we must also say that that yes contains a very real no to the ways we hurt each other, to the ways we wound our world, and to the part of each of us that is self-destructive. It also says no to our need to manipulate instead of cherish, to control life instead of letting it unfold. This reminds me of Eliot's image of the wounded surgeon and Henri Nouwen's image of the wounded healer. Jesus is the skilled physician, the wounded surgeon. We need operations, both tiny and large, and we might have to take some large unpleasant pills. But after each pill, we feel better. And after each operation, we feel more knit together, more whole, and more truly ourselves.

God speaks a major yes to our world, but within that yes is a no, and that is for the sake of the yes. If we do not acknowledge this, then God's love, as we speak of it, is more like the love of Santa Claus, more like the tranquilizer that blocks out our pain or the amphetamine that can keep us high and excited and constantly jolly.

By ourselves we cannot patch up the wounds that sin brings. There is but one remedy for sin: God's overwhelming forgiveness. He waits to greet us like the father waiting to greet the prodigal son. He wants to take us in his arms and cradle us like the shepherd cradles the lost sheep. He wants us to leap into his forgiving, loving arms.

Our problem is that we are afraid to look at our sinfulness. We don't fully understand how intensely God is ready to forgive us. God is eager to forgive us. As the parable in Matthew instructs, there is more joy in heaven over one sinner who repents "than over ninety-nine that never went astray" (Matt. 18:13).

Another part of the mystery of forgiveness is that if we acknowledge our sin and receive God's forgiveness, a deeper love, a deeper compassion grows in our hearts. Jesus said of the prostitute "Her sins, which are many, are forgiven, for she has loved much; but he who is forgiven little, loves little" (Luke 7:47).

In asking forgiveness we become vulnerable, woundable. We have to acknowledge that we don't have everything under control; we have to acknowledge the depth of our need. When we do this, when we receive the tender forgiveness of the Father, this deepens and escalates our capacity to love. As the apostle Paul said, "Where sin increased, grace abounded all the more" (Rom. 5:20).

The following is a prayer script that will help you remember the ways God has forgiven you. A sense of being forgiven leaves us feeling bright, clean, and refreshed. Remembering those times of forgiveness strengthens our thankfulness and makes it easier for us to turn to God when our selfishness again puts up barriers. Remembering God's mercy can be a constant source for a deepening and ever-increasing compassion, a source of deep at-homeness with yourself, a source of a great ability to accept and forgive others.

PRAYER EXPERIENCE

PART I

Relax. Rest in God's love. When you are relaxed and resting in the love of God, let your mind remember times that you have experienced forgiveness. Perhaps this was during and after the Sacrament of Reconciliation, perhaps when you felt the unexpected forgiveness of a family member whom you had hurt. Perhaps it was when you overcame a serious problem through God's forgiveness. Let your mind float back to the peace of those times. Center on the sense of at-homeness and peace.

PART II

After you have experienced the joyful memories of the grace of forgiveness in times past, you are ready to experience forgiveness in the present.

Relax. Repeat a short prayer phrase for a few moments. Become aware of your body, your emotions, your thoughts. Pause and ask God to bring to awareness one or more ways you have been putting yourself first in ways that harm others, God, or yourself. In your own words ask his forgiveness. Sense the loving peace of his healing light surround you. Bathe in that healing light as long as you wish.

If you belong to a sacramental church, celebrate and seal God's forgiveness in the Sacrament of Reconciliation.

SCRIPTURE JOURNEY

So, he told them this parable: "What man of you, having a hundred sheep, if he has lost one of them, does not leave the ninety-nine in the wilderness, and go after the one which is lost, until he finds it? And when he has found it, he lays it on his shoulders, rejoicing. And when he comes home, he calls together his friends and his neighbors, saying to them, 'Rejoice with me, for I have found my sheep which was lost.'

"And he arose and came to his father. But while he was yet at a distance, his father saw him and had compassion and ran and embraced him and kissed him. And the son said to him, 'Father, I have sinned against heaven and before you; I am no longer worthy to be called your son.' But his father said to his servants, 'Bring quickly the best robe and put it on him; and put a ring on his hand and shoes on his feet; and bring the fatted calf and kill it, and let us eat and make merry; for this my son was dead, and is alive again; he was lost, and is found.' And they began to make merry."

(LUKE 15:3–6, 20–24)

Imagine that you are the shepherd. You leave the flock to hunt the lone frightened lamb that has lost its way and is now on a cliff high on a hill, frightened to come down on its own. The lamb is crying out as though crying for its mother. You can hear the desperation in that cry. You soothe and stroke the lamb. You speak soft words and you see the lamb's muscles loosen up and calmness return. The lamb nuzzles you with its head. You pick the lamb up and put it on your shoulder. What are your feelings? A scene like this is one of tenderness, of warmth, of compassion, of joy. Allow yourself to feel the tenderness of the lamb on your neck as you bring it back.

Now shift your imagination to a new scene. In this scene you are the father, the one who has been misused and poorly treated by the "prodigal" son. You are the one who grieved for the son with worried anguish. Now you see him, now you begin running to him. He is disheveled, covered with dirt; he hangs his head as he walks. You run to him and throw your arms around him. You share with him your gladness and the two of you then experience the joy of the celebration.

These scenes give you a glimpse of the compassion that God feels toward his children. Where you are seated now, have a sense of Jesus coming up behind you, putting his arms around you. Feel the touch of his hand on yours. Now you know that your coming to him with your lostness gives him joy, joy such as you experienced when you were the shepherd, joy such as you experienced when you were like the father in the story. Just let him hold you there for a moment. Linger and repose in his shining love.

PART THREE

God's Love Opens
New Dimensions

12

A LOVE THAT GIVES BIRTH TO WONDER

Mark was a person whose plans seemed always to succeed. A superb athlete in high school, he helped carry his team to the state finals. He was a straight-A student and yet he was popular at the same time. He came from one of those rare homes that seemed to be free of major problems. His parents always let their children express their feelings and opinions. Mark exuded healthiness.

A bout with hepatitis when he was fourteen, an illness that nearly took his life, somehow deepened him. He could talk with bright eyes about the latest pop music, loved to go to dances, yet he always took time each night to read the Bible and say a short prayer.

When I met Mark, he was a senior in college. He told me that his life had begun to seem dry. Something was missing. Although his degree in engineering and his excellent record in college would guarantee him a high-paying job, he had been struggling for months with a decision to spend two years in Latin America as a lay volunteer. He attended one of our twilight retreats and talked to me afterward. He said that the whole idea of meditative and contemplative prayer seemed to open new horizons for him.

Mark was a person who loved to get into things and do them well and thoroughly. He began to do something that is very rare in healthy young people: he started taking an hour a day for prayer. He would stop by the campus church after his last class and spend an hour there every day. One night several weeks later, while he was studying, a deep sense of resting in God's love came over him, a sense of being cradled in a tingling, vibrant love that warmed him to the very core of his being. Warm currents flowed through his body and a deep stillness settled in. In the gentlest of transitions, a beautiful light filled the room; a dazzling light surrounded him. Mute with wonder, he was totally immersed in brightness, warmth, and peace, bathed in emotions of joy, rapture, and reverential awe. It was as though senses new within him awakened. It was a timeless moment. His eyes brimmed with tears. He stayed there in the midst of the light for twenty or thirty minutes, weeping because of the peace that came over him. The light gradually faded, but he sat there most of the night, awake, resting in peacefulness.

In the following weeks, Mark kept up his hour of prayer and said a strong yes to the two years of missionary work. He wanted to give to others some of the goodness that had been given to him. Experiences such as Mark's are far more common than we realize. You cannot will such an experience; you cannot choose when such a timeless moment comes. It comes as a gracious gift, and it comes with God's timing.

Mark was wise, too, not to make more of the experience than warranted. He knew that it is the steady encounter of God in our daily lives that counts. Although experiences such as Mark's can widen us, give us hope, nudge us on a bit, I don't think it is wise to seek after them in their own right. Such religious experiences are usually a by-product of our everyday experience of God. There is always a strong human element in such graced times. Our unconscious plays a very clear role. This side of glory no one has a "direct line." Revelation ended with Jesus Christ. Yet, of course, God can be very much in such times, as he is in all aspects of our living and feeling. We seek the experience of God, not the God of experiences.

Marriage helps illustrate this. Giddy feelings of falling in love can come to a couple at many times during their marriage, or during their courtship. The feelings of being close come when couples genuinely share their feelings, forgiving one another, acknowledging their anger if they need to.

And so it is with God. We don't look for the feeling of closeness by itself. What we seek are lives that are informed by the gospel, changed by the gospel to move in the right direction. We talk about such powerful religious experiences because they are part of the landscape. We should neither repress them nor give them undue importance.

God's love transcends our logical knowledge. When we open ourselves to him, we open ourselves to the dimension of the wondrous, to the spiritual world, to an experience beyond words. When I think of wonder, I think of children two to five years old. The sense of life's mystery has not been bleached out of them. They take a leaf, hold it in their hands, delight in it; they grab a spring flower and giggle with joy. Just watching a train go by becomes an adventure. Society educates much of the sense of wonder out of us, but when we open ourselves to God's love, to prayer, wonder is reborn in us.

In his moving novel, *Creek Mary's Blood,* Dee Brown tells the story of a Cherokee Indian who entered into the wonder of the spiritual world. The book is the *Gone with the Wind* of the American Indians. Part of the story involves a well-educated Cherokee named Dane who acted as a scout for wagon trains moving West. Later he married a Cheyenne and joined the Cheyenne tribe. The Cheyenne religion, like much North American Indian spirituality, resembles Christian spirituality.

An important event in Dane's life was his entry into what he called "the real world." By this he meant the spiritual world—the dimension of the wondrous. Describing his spiritual discovery to a reporter, Dane said:

"I lived with the Cheyenne a long time before I learned how to cross into the real world, and all that time my wife and children could do this and they were puzzled because I could not join them there. . . . I was finally able to find my way into the real world with my family. I discovered mysterious powers within my memory and learned that when you pray for others to become strong you become strong, too, because that connects you with everything else. You become a part of everything and that is how I knew that I was necessary to my family and they were necessary to me. . . ."

"What is it like, the real world?" the reporter asked.

He remained silent for a while and then spoke slowly.

"Being a man who loves words, I have often thought about that. But some things cannot be put into words. The closest I ever came was an English word. Shimmering."

"Shimmering?"

"Yes, like swimming in moonlight."

SCRIPTURE JOURNEY

We are going to enter a scene from the Bible you have probably read about many times: the scene from the sixth chapter of Isaiah, which records Isaiah's vision in the temple when he saw the Lord in all his majesty and glory.

In the year that King Uzziah died I saw the Lord sitting upon a throne, high and lifted up; and his train filled the temple. Above him stood the seraphim; each had six wings: with two, he covered his face, and with two he covered his feet, and with two he flew. And one called to another and said:

"Holy, holy, holy is the Lord of hosts; and the whole earth is full of his glory."

And the foundations of the thresholds shook at the voice of him who called, and the house was filled with smoke. And I said; "Woe is me! For I am lost; for I am a man of unclean lips, and I dwell in the midst of a people of unclean lips; for my eyes have seen the King, the Lord of hosts!"

Then flew one of the seraphim to me, having in his hand a burning coal which he had taken with tongs from the altar. And he touched my mouth and said, "Behold, this has touched your lips; your guilt is taken away, and your sin forgiven." And I heard the voice of the Lord saying, "Whom shall I send, and who will go for us?" Then I said, "Here am I! Send me."

(ISA. 6:1–8)

The time is not now; the time is that period in ancient Israel. It's a glorious day and the sun shines brightly. You are standing outside the temple—a huge churchlike building. A man dressed in ancient clothes comes out of the temple. His facial muscles are at ease, loose and relaxed, emanating a radiant glow. His eyes sparkle brightly, full of wonder and mystery. This is Isaiah and he had just emerged from an overwhelming experience of the Lord, the experience you have just read about.

Isaiah looks at you and says simply, "Now it is your turn."

You slowly enter the temple. There is no need to picture exactly what the temple is like; just go in and find a comfortable seat.

Perhaps you feel some fear, some puzzlement. You sense you will encounter the same majestic presence, the same overwhelming vision that Isaiah has just experienced. You know that such an experience can awaken abilities and gifts that are buried inside you, abilities to sense and feel that you have never used before. Wherever the Lord is, wherever God's love is, there is also ease and peace and warmth and tender kindness for those who open their hearts to him.

Close your eyes. The scene that is about to unfold is not one that you can picture fully with your conscious mind. Just having a vague sense of that scene taking place before you is enough. Your eyes are closed now, and after a moment you become aware that the Lord is in the temple, sitting on his throne, high and lifted up. His train, his robe fills the temple. Above him stand the seraphim; one calls out, "Holy, holy, holy is the Lord of hosts; the whole earth is full of his glory."

You bask in a tender awe, a hushed wonder. Let the wonder and awe begin to sink into you, flowing through your skin into your deepest self. There is no need to intensify or try to feel the feelings; just have a sense of the feelings inherent in such a scene, a vague sense that these feelings of wonder and awe are like a cloud or other airy substance sinking into your depths. The feelings will come at the time that's right for you. Perhaps later as you go about your daily life, your unconscious may release powerful images that help you taste and drink in the scene.

You hear the loud call of the seraph reverberating in the temple: "Holy, holy, holy is the Lord of hosts; the whole earth is full of his glory." You can feel the vibrations of the loud voice going up through your legs, through all of you. To be in the midst of such a scene, perhaps like Isaiah, you feel a great sense of unworthiness and fear. Do you? What are some things in your daily life that make you fearful? Just become aware of those feelings; there is no need to judge.

One of the seraphim puts a hot coal in your mouth. You feel the coal in your mouth. Instead of a searing, burning pain, you feel gentle warmth that surprises you. The gentle and firm warmth from the coal spreads down through your throat, cleansing you. It flows farther down, into your heart, expanding into a ball of glowing, warming light within your heart. It goes down your spine, warming, cleansing, healing. Reaching the base of your spine, it brings the tingling warmth there, too. You feel purified all over by the burning coal.

The Lord says to you, "Whom shall I send? And who will go?" See if you, like Isaiah, are able to say yes to that request. If you are, move your lips and say, "I will go, Lord. Send me."

In doing this meditation, do not struggle to feel any particular feelings. The meditation is designed to prime and open up your heart so that your unconscious can pour forth feelings and insights later. During the actual meditation, you may feel dry. Yet the next day or the next week, you may find yourself tasting a fiery awe in everyday life, feeling the wonder of God, experiencing a new humility, a new purity, a new cleansing.

13

NATURE—A PATHWAY FOR GOD'S LOVE

Scenes and sounds from nature are bright threads woven throughout the cloth of Scripture. It seems as though the biblical writers cannot speak of God without using images and comparisons from nature. "I will lift up my eyes to the hills, from whence comes my help. My help comes from the Lord" (Ps. 21:1). "As the mountains are round about Jerusalem, so the Lord is round about his people" (Ps. 125:2). "Bless the Lord, O my soul! O Lord my God, you are very great! You are clothed with honor and majesty." You "cover yourself with light as with a garment." You "make the clouds your chariot" and "ride on the wings of the wind." You "make the winds your messengers, fire and flame your ministers." You "make springs gush forth in the valleys; they flow between the hills (Ps. 104:10).

As the sensitive, God-filled poet Gerard Manley Hopkins tells us: "The world is charged with grandeur of God. It will flame out, like shining from shook foil; it gathers to a greatness, like the ooze of oil. . . . Because the Holy Ghost over the bent world broods with warm breast and with ah! bright wings."

Bonaventure wrote: "In creation we see the footprints of God." Nature can be a source, a channel for God's presence coming to us. Remembering nature expands our capacity for experiencing God every day in his creation.

PRAYER EXPERIENCE

When you are relaxed, prayerful, and in the loving presence of God, begin to imagine some of the beautiful scenes of nature you have seen: sunrises, sunsets, the hot beating sun coming down on you in summertime, the sound and sight of waves crashing against the sand, the sky at night, the smell of raindrops on a dusty sidewalk, the fresh air of high mountains, the beauty of mountains against the sky—special times in nature. Relive such times in your imagination—taste, sights, scents, sounds. Relive the emotions; feel them again.

Remember a nature spot that is special to you. Go there in your imagination. Relax there for awhile and allow that scene to express God's love to you.

SCRIPTURE JOURNEY

When Jesus prayed, he went out to be with nature. Whenever he needed refreshment, whenever he needed healing, whenever he needed deep communion with the Father, he went away to the hills and the water. As someone of Indian descent, I know how much of God's healing comes through his creation around us. Jesus knew that, too. Such phrases as "Look at the birds in the sky, the lilies of the field" fill his speech. All his imagery, his words show a profound communion with creation. The two main characteristics of Jesus' prayer were his *"abba"* experience of the love of the Father and his communion with creation all around him. That sensitivity to nature shows itself in his style of speaking.

In these days he went out into the hills to pray; and all night he continued in prayer to God.

(LUKE 6:12)

In your imagination, go to the Palestine of Jesus' time. Place yourself beside him on a mountain, where he will pray all night. Sit there on a rock. He becomes aware of the vast and glorious array of stars on this quiet night. There seem to be millions of them, glittering brightly in the sky. They shine out in every direction through the immense expanses of the universe. They speak of an infinite calm that is rich with wonder.

You can see the lights of the towns below and hear the gentle lapping of the water against the shore. You sit near Jesus and it is all right to experience with him the healing that comes through creation. Jesus enters into a reverential awe as he opens to the world around him: the nighttime sounds of insects, the glowing moon, and the sounds of the lake below. You sense a gentle stillness come over him, a warm human stillness, an inexpressible stillness tinged with wonder. At the very same time, mixed with these emotions, is a letting go of pain, of tension, of hurt into the heart of the Father. He drinks in the love of the Father that comes to him in the bosom of his own heart, the love of the Father that flows to him through the sparkling beauty of nature. How easy it is to feel what he is feeling. You can sense the movement of prayer within him, a quietness so profound that it soothes and comforts as it connects him with the Father.

You know it's all right for you to draw nearer, to draw so very near. You move close beside him. It is as though the air around him is thick with love and prayer, and the letting go of hurt. You feel safe, so very safe that you reach out and touch his robe. Hold tightly to the robe and allow the love-filled stillness of Jesus' prayer to flow through your hand, to your heart, to your whole body. Experience that wordless sense of communion with the Father and with nature that is taking place in him right now.

14

THE KINDLY LIGHT
THAT HEALS

She came up to me just after I dismissed the group for lunch. She was middle-aged, well dressed, with a poise that bespoke her education and background. But a stark and vivid fear glinted in her eyes and her brow was creased with worry. Hesitantly, she told her story. Several weeks before, her husband, a high school teacher, had been arrested for child molestation. Her world was collapsing around her. My friend Robert joined us and as we both listened it was clear that there was no easy solution. In the short time that we would have with her there was no way that we could help her sort out all the issues and all the feelings. So we did what we could: we sat and listened.

Then Robert suggested that we join hands in a conversational prayer. The room was still thick with the presence of God from the prayer time we had just finished with the group, so it was easy for us to move into prayer. In our prayer, the three of us gave the situation to Jesus. We knew there was no instant solution. We just asked that he be with her in the hurting and that he help her find supportive friends.

After we finished our conversational prayer, we drifted farther into the healing stillness that surrounded us and stayed there awhile. When we came out of that quiet, she shared with us that in her deep imagination, she pictured herself on a small island in the midst of a surging, flowing river. It was wintertime and the water was full of ice. That was for her an apt image of her feelings and her situation. Then she said, "I saw around myself on that island the healing glow of God's love, and Jesus standing beside me. I knew then," she said, "that Jesus was with me, even in the midst of my deep troubles and confusion." As she spoke, tears glistened on her pale face. She knew she still faced agonizing and unsettling times. She knew there were no magic solutions. But she left that day with the knowledge that God would be with her in the immense and terrible agony she would go through.

Light imagery permeates Christian writing and prayer. References to light fill the Scriptures, particularly the Psalms. "Your word is a lamp to my feet and a light to my path" (Ps. 119:105).

The shekinah presence of the Lord in the form of light guarded the children of Israel in their exodus of liberation from Egypt. In the New Testament, light surrounded Jesus on Mt. Tabor. Light poured down on Paul when he fell off the horse during his conversion. Second Corinthians says that we behold the splendor of God shining on the face of Jesus.

Throughout the Christian centuries, light metaphors and the actual experience of "inner light" have been a basic part of Christian spiritual teaching. The Anglican poet Henry Vaughan, author of the loveliest of the seventeenth-century devotional poems, constantly speaks of experiencing God through light. In his well-known poem "The World," he says:

> I saw Eternity the other night like a great ring of pure
> and endless light. All calm as it was bright.

Jakob Böhme, German Protestant spiritual writer of the seventeenth century, speaks of "inward light," "God's Light in the Soul," and "the Light of the Majesty." Evelyn Underhill in her classic book *Mysticism* documents light in the prayer experiences of the great Christian saints and herself calls this inward light "that light whose smile kindles the Universe."

LIGHT—A WAY OF PRAYING

Light is more than a metaphor; it can also be a way of praying. Jakob Böhme prayed by focusing on a spot of light reflected from a crystal drinking glass. Architects designed Gothic cathedrals so that multicolored light flooded the faithful. Eastern Orthodox churches evoke the wonder of divine Light with scores of candles reflecting off shiny gold and silver icons.

St. Seraphim of Sarov, the gentle "nature saint" who has been called the Russian St. Francis, suggests imagining light as a way of praying:

> . . . a man should shut his eyes and concentrate on bringing his mind down into the depths of his heart, ardently calling on the name of our Lord Jesus Christ. . . . When the mind is concentrated in the heart through this exercise, then the light of Christ begins to shine, lighting up the temple of the soul with its divine radiance. . . . When a man contemplates this eternal light within him his mind remains pure.

Many of the meditations in this book use light imagery. It is a basic building block in imagination prayer.

PRAYER EXPERIENCE

PART I

Take time to relax and be still. Repeat a short prayer phrase. Picture yourself surrounded by God's presence in the form of an egg-shaped oval of light that encircles you. If your imagination is fuzzy today, just have the sense that you are surrounded by invisible light. You don't have to picture the light with precision to enter into the mystery of it. A sense of being surrounded by light is enough.

The warm light of God's love absorbs your fears, anger, and negativity like a sponge. The light richly relaxes and refreshes you. You tingle with newness. The light tells you in a beautiful, eternal way, a way beyond words, of God's immense, unfathomable, tender, and special love for you. Rest for a long time, sensing yourself bathed in his light.

PART II

When you have become comfortable using the first meditation, you can follow it with this second meditation. Go through the first meditation—relaxing, picturing yourself surrounded by an oval light. Rest in that light.

After you are comfortable in the light, begin to be aware of your breathing, your breathing in and your breathing out. The word for the Holy Spirit in Scripture is also the word for *breathe*. Allow your breathing in and out to remind you of the Holy Spirit. Just notice your breathing.

Now have a sense every time you breathe in that you are breathing in the light that surrounds you. As you breathe it in, a warm, glowing center grows in the depths of your chest, warming your heart. The more you breathe in the light, the more the center of your chest glows, relaxing you, healing you, warming your being with God's love. Each time you exhale, have a sense that you are breathing out negativity and fear. Each time you inhale, you are breathing in light.

Take as long as you like breathing in the love of God.

PART III

You may want to go even farther with this light meditation. So many of our emotions, positive and negative, are located in the muscles of our bodies. Now take this light and in your imagination breathe the light down to your feet. Feel your feet filled with the love of God. Breathe the light down to your calves. Fill them up with the love of God. Breathe the light down to your thighs. Fill them up with the love of God. Breathe the light down to your genitals. Fill them with the love of God.

SCRIPTURE JOURNEY

A soul-stirring Greek icon of the transfiguration hangs in a permanent place in my bedroom. According to Eastern Christians, there comes a time in many people's lives when they experience the light of Mt. Tabor as a call onward into the love of God. In this prayer experience you will follow Peter, James, and John up Mt. Tabor. If your Bible contains pictures of the transfiguration, you might look at those before you begin this meditation.

And after six days Jesus took with him Peter and James and John his brother, and led them up a high mountain apart. And he was transfigured before them, and his face shone like the sun, and his garments became white as the light. And behold, there appeared to them Moses and Elijah, talking with him. And Peter said to Jesus, "Lord, it is well that we are here; if you wish, I will make three booths here, one for you and one for Moses and one for Elijah." He was still speaking, when lo, a bright cloud overshadowed them, and a voice from the cloud, said, "This is my beloved Son, with whom I am well pleased; listen to him." When the disciples heard this, they fell on their faces, and were filled with awe. But Jesus came and touched them, saying, "Rise, and have no fear." And when they lifted up their eyes, they saw no one, but Jesus only.

(MATT. 17:1–8)

In your imagination you are standing with Peter, James, and John. You behold Jesus; "his face shines like the sun, and his garments are white as light." Your unconscious knows how much of that scene is right for you to see right now. Your deep heart knows very well how to listen to the stirrings of the Holy Spirit. The light bathing Jesus is like no other light. Immense, radiant love shines forth from his face. Let that brightness warm you, heal you, and wash over your heart. Stay there for awhile and hear Jesus say to you, "Rise and have no fear."

15

EXPERIENCING THE VASTNESS OF GOD'S LOVE

A powerful image in the Christian tradition for experiencing the vastness of God's love has been the ocean or the sea. As John Wesley put it, "We lose ourselves in the ocean of divinity." Or as the contemporary hymn says, "There is a wideness in God's mercy like the wideness of the sea."

PRAYER EXPERIENCE

Take a few minutes to relax. Imagine that you are in a wondrous place, a special place. You are on a huge, beautiful beach of white powdery sand. A vast ocean stretches out before you. You are lying on the beach with your feet in the water. Hear the sound of the crashing whitecaps. Smell the salt air as it fills your nostrils. Hear the gulls squawking as they glide high above the sea.

The water is warm. The waves begin to break over you. You realize that this is a special ocean; this is the ocean of God's love. It is endless. Feel the waves breaking over your whole body, one after the other. The water is warm and healing. It is as though the waves flow not only on your outside but on your inside too. They go right through you, their gentle motion carrying away anxiety, tension. Each wave fills you with joy. Those waves tell you without words of God's love. They leave you deeply peaceful.

Rest for as long as you wish on the beach, allowing the waves of God's love to sweep over you and heal you.

SCRIPTURE JOURNEY

For this reason, I bow my knees before the Father, from whom every family in heaven and on earth is named, that according to the riches of his glory, He may grant you to be strengthened with night through his spirit in the inner man, and that Christ may dwell in your hearts through faith; that you, will be rooted and grounded in love, may have the power to comprehend with all the saints what is the breadth and length and height and depth, and to know the love of Christ which surpasses knowledge, that you may be filled with the fullness of God.

(EPH. 3:14–19)

You are standing atop a high mountain. As you look through the clouds below, you see a limitless canyon, a vast abyss. No one can measure its height or depth. You stand in amazement at the scene below you.

You glimpse the beginnings of gentle white light. You sense someone moving toward you—someone who emanates safety, security, and wonder. An angel steps before you. As he takes your hand, your heart swells with wonder and comfort and safety. You stand there awhile, drifting even further into calmness. The clouds begin to glitter with a sparkling light, a light that dazzles you and warms you at the same time. You hold your breath in awe. You sense what the angel wants you to do. He wants you to jump with him into the vast canyon below, the canyon of the height and depth of Christ's love.

What do you feel as you contemplate jumping into the canyon? Perhaps fear—fear of the unknown. Perhaps worry—worry that if you are surrounded by so much love, you will cease to be you. Possibly mixed in with those feelings is a yearning, a longing for the ineffable and inconceivable love that awaits you down below.

Don't jump until you are ready. When you jump, you feel so light that you float through the sparkling clouds with the angel. Ways of feeling, ways of seeing that have always been within you but unknown to you come alive. You sense a love that is beyond all telling, a measureless joy, a vibrant aliveness that cannot be expressed in words. A sweetness fills the inner spaces of your heart. The light is so bright that you close your eyes, and still the light shines through your closed eyelids. How easy it is to feel amazed at a time like this. It's easy to feel the energy that amazement brings—tingling energy, bright, sparkling energy. And how weightless and free you feel floating in this endless cloud of light.

As you float, the deep clouds pass on to you the love of Jesus. As you breathe in the light that sparkles and startles and amazes you, the loving energy flows to every cell of your body. Every cell feels vibrantly alive. You are bathed in a heavenly glow. You float toward the center, the very center of Christ's love, toward this light beyond all light. In this place of bright stillness beyond all stillness, of infinite love and glowing warmth, you rest—settling in there in the center, growing calm there, being filled mightily in your inner self.

16

JESUS SHOWS YOU THE WAY TO THE FATHER

Most fourteen-year-olds don't read Voltaire or Thomas Paine and have their faith shaken, but I did. Most fourteen-year-olds don't read T. S. Eliot but I did. I have always surrounded myself with books. When I reach back to my earliest memories, I see myself as a toddler amid a bedful of picture books that my mother read to me. Throughout my life I have let books carry me to faraway places and new ideas.

In the early sixties, my high school years, the books I read led me away from faith. That era vibrated with a giddy confidence in the ability of science and progress to bring positive change. Harvey Cox would later call it the "secular city." The infinite loving mystery we name when we say the word *God* had little room in a world in which we thought science would explain every unknown and solve every problem. Yet, I desperately wanted God to be there. I yearned for the consolation that faith brings. But I possessed a rigorous intellectual honesty at a very early age, and I have always been "blessed" or "afflicted" with the need to look at things from all viewpoints. In those teenage years, when I so wanted the warmth and the healing and consolation that come from knowing God, uncertainty tossed me about.

Even in the midst of all that uncertainty, I discovered the Christian poet T. S. Eliot, and the stirrings of faith that filled his later poems tugged at my heart. As part of my searching I began to attend Edgewood Presbyterian Church in my hometown of Columbus, Georgia. The pastor there, Ernie Gilmore, had a thorough intellectual and theological knowledge of Christianity along with a warm-hearted faith. He spent long hours with me listening to my uncertainties and giving me books to read by C. S. Lewis and Karl Barth. About this time, Roy and Revell Hession, two English laypeople who have written many spiritual books, came to conduct a week of renewal at the church. After one session, Roy Hession came to the pew and talked to me.

Roy's whole being emanated gentleness, sensitivity, and a deeply held faith that warmed him deep within. I poured out my heart to him. I said I wanted so much to know Jesus, but that I had enormous intellectual uncertainties and that I could not, by an act of will, make those uncertainties go away. He was very pleasant as he listened, and then he said "Your yearning is faith." He said that faith is always that, just faith—as it says in Hebrews, "Faith is the evidence of things unseen." Uncertainties are the other side of faith. He explained that faith is not making ourselves certain of ideas but taking our hearts and personalities, our whole selves, as we are, where we are, to God; that faith is coming to God and handing our lives over to him, even if we are uncertain. With a bit of humor, he told me about the agnostic's prayer: "Oh God, if there is a God, save my soul, if I have a soul." And he suggested I pray a prayer that went something like this: "Oh Lord, I want you to be there but I can't be sure that you're there. I give myself to you. I give my life to you, as I am, where I am, with all my uncertainties."

I did not experience a powerful light as St. Paul did or a strange warming of my heart as did John Wesley. I just experienced a sense of rightness in the prayer, a sense that I had been developing faith all along and that it was time to profess my faith and join the church. Over the next few months, my heart slowly developed a gentle awareness of the felt presence of God.

The desire to teach and to preach stirred in my heart. The Presbyterian church received me as a candidate for the ministry and I went to Belhaven College in Jackson, Mississippi, to pursue my studies. There I received superb training from evangelical Presbyterians in Scripture, exegesis, and philosophy. The religion faculty were top-notch. Their advanced degrees came from Edinburgh, Oxford, and Cambridge. They were solid men who not only taught us but also loved us. Their example created a family-like atmosphere among the students. My time there was a time of nurture, learning how to have friends and be a friend, learning how to love my fellow students and deal with relationships. It was a blessed time because that nuture gave me the security to begin following my heart's yearning even further. My heart hungered for prayer, deep prayer, and I sensed the Catholic church had wisdom on prayer. I met Cardinal Bernard Law, who was then a young priest in Jackson. We became close friends, and he became a mentor and spiritual father. There was something very profound about him. He possessed a wholeness, an at-homeness with himself and with the world, a holy joy. After graduating from Belhaven, I went on to postgraduate study at Union Theological Seminary in Richmond, Virginia.

As I look back over the last ten years, I find that it has been a graced time for me, a time of love and joy, a time of adventure. Many mornings I awaken with a tingling excitement for the day before me, and many nights as I go to sleep a gratitude bubbles for the day I have been through. Yes, there are still some dreary times—we all have those. Yes, there are times of strain with my friends. But even in the midst of the daily struggles we all face, my life throbs with meaning and direction. So it is hard for me, as I think back to the late sixties and early seventies, my time at theology school, to recall how dismal life seemed for me then.

For me the darkest time came during those three years after Belhaven, when I was doing my graduate work in theology at Union Theological Seminary and Austin Seminary. The problem was not the schools; the problem was inside me. We had good professors who made it known that they wanted to be our friends, not just our teachers. There were many decent and caring people among the students. But I developed a very deep depression. The nauseating depths of despair became my constant companion. Just putting one foot in front of the other took struggle and willpower. I had no energy. I lost interest in people and in any sort of recreation. I sat in my room, sometimes for twelve hours at a time. It was a struggle just to get up and go to class. Despite my absences, I did well on tests and even shined on some of the hardest research papers. I didn't reach my potential, of course, but I was a solid student.

I still do not fully know the reason for this depression. A major part, I know, was that I pushed my feelings deep down within me—I lived in my head, not my heart. Also, I had never grieved for Pop, my grandfather. I had repressed my feelings of loss and, in doing that, had hidden away my Indian heritage as well as my memories of Pop. Physical illness caused many of the symptoms, I'm sure. I continually had the dragged-out feelings that come with flu, though there were no outward signs of the illness. Some time after I left seminary, my doctor discovered that I had cholecystitis, a chronic, low-grade gallbladder infection that surgery eventually cured. I also struggled with the deep calling in my heart to become Catholic. I transferred to Austin Theological Seminary and my depression deepened in my last year, affecting my academic performance. A sleepiness over which I had no control would overtake me. At times, I would sleep eighteen hours a day. Coffee, exercise, nothing would banish that sleepiness. I was utterly powerless to change any of this and deeply ashamed. I had no self-esteem left. In my mind I was letting down my family, the church, and everyone who loved me. And nothing seemed to help.

A deceptive calmness masked my inner turmoil. In addition to my own inner agony, I had to deal with the frustration and justifiable anger of my professors and friends. Instead of returning after my third year in theology, I took a year off to work as a volunteer at the Well, a campus ministry to the University of Texas. I hoped being away from the pressure of school would help ease my depression, but it didn't. I had tried counseling and one of my professors, Rod Williams, had become a strong, supportive friend in my struggles, another spiritual father.

Nothing seemed to work. One day I picked up a book by Thomas Merton called *Contemplative Prayer*. I understood little of what Merton was talking about, but I knew he was speaking out of a dimension of wholeness, a dimension of the experience of God for which I hungered. The book moved me so much that I drove fifteen hours to the newly opened monastery in Pecos, New Mexico, where I spoke with the abbot, Fr. David Gareats. I said, "I have come here to learn how to meditate. Can you show me how?" He smiled, and said, "Not in this one-hour appointment, I can't. But I can give you some books." He loaded me up with the writings of the church fathers and a host of books on historical spirituality.

When I decide to do something, I rarely do it half-heartedly. On returning to Austin, I devoured the books and began to spend several hours a day in the type of meditative prayer I was learning from them. Even after these weeks of meditation, my prayer was as dry as desert sands. I was still deeply mired in depression. Yet I did begin to feel some movement within, a whispering, an impelling, a quiet and powerful happening in the depths of my soul. It brought no relief or consolation yet, but I knew something was stirring.

One evening, I found the pain inside especially weighty, like a ball of lead. I went upstairs to the top floor of the Well. Windows on every side were open to the springtime air. The pain inside hurt so. I sat on the floor and rocked back and forth. I said, "Oh, Lord, I hurt, I hurt so bad. I don't know why I hurt. I just know I hurt." Finally I began feeling the emotions I had so long denied. The sobs began to come, racking sobs from below my ribs. The pain filled me, till it seemed that I was no more me but that I was all pain. As the sobs poured out of me, the stream of pain seemed endless. After the sobs were through, though, my mind was clear for awhile. I felt very tired but the weight of the hurting inside me had lightened. I was refreshed; I began to sense something new slowly coming. I fell asleep there on the carpet and slept all night.

The next morning when I awoke the world was bright. I had never known such brightness. It was a beautiful day and it moved my heart. It was as though my heart reached out and took in all this bright fullness—the green trees, the fresh air, I breathed it in and drank it in. And even as I looked out upon it, it was as though the beauty there melted into a new dimension. I knew that God was in my heart. What a fresh time it was for me! I drove into the country where the hills were covered in carpets of newly blooming bluebonnets. God's nearness filled my body with warming light, nourished me, cradled me, carrying me into a tranquil calm. That time of wonder and newness lasted several weeks. During that time, I didn't want to miss anything. I wanted to taste it all, savor all aspects of creation around me. I registered every sight, smell, and taste of those weeks.

Like all such experiences this side of glory, it faded. The depression returned but it was profoundly lessened. Even though it would be years before the depression left for good, the bright water of hope flowed within.

I knew, too, that it was time for me to enter the Catholic church. Fr. Bernie Law, on a visit to Jackson, received me into the church. Usually it's best for us to bloom where we are planted, but there are exceptions, and I was an exception. The Presbyterian church had been good to me and it will always be a part of me. I did not leave behind the things I had believed; I just added some things. The ringing of those mighty Reformation hymns, the centrality of Christ and Scripture, the emphasis on the triumph of grace will always be a part of me.

Through all my journey, one theme emerges: Jesus leading me to the Father.

In this meditation you imagine Jesus. Imagining Jesus is a very traditional way of approaching God. The following meditation knits together many of the images we have already used into a synthesis, a whole.

PRAYER EXPERIENCE

PART I

Relax. Enter deeply into the restfulness of God's love.

Gently, now, I would like for you to picture yourself in a beautiful meadow, the meadow of the Twenty-third Psalm. It's springtime. The grass is green. The sky is clear and blue. Beautiful trees surround you. There is a stream gurgling into a quiet pond. You lie on the grass taking a sunbath. It is a special place, God's place. The warm sunlight beams down on you. It is the sunlight of God's own love. Just lie there, taking a sunbath in God's love. Allow his healing sunlight to restore you. Remain in the sunlight of his love as long as you wish.

This light leaves you feeling fresh, clean. You have never felt so good, so much in awe of God's creation, so much in wonder at God himself. You marvel at the beauty of God's creation all around you—the trees, the birds, the stream. Hear the rustle of the grass.

PART II

Someone is moving toward you in bare feet. A sense of fear and awe comes over you. You stand up and look and there is Jesus. Picture him any way you would like.

At first, when you look at him you have a sense of your unworthiness, of the bad things you've done in your life. But you look into his eyes and they are full of untellable love. His eyes say, "I love you, I care for you. It's all right. I'm burning with love for you from all eternity." His eyes bring deep forgiveness and peace and unspeakable joy to you. He embraces you. Feel his arms tenderly and tightly around you. Rest in his embrace for as long as you wish.

PART III

Jesus passes from being in your arms to being in your heart—from a physical presence to a spiritual one. Feel him in your heart.

He speaks to you from the depth of your heart. "I will show you the love of the Father." After he has said this, you feel yourself getting lighter and lighter. You are so light you begin to float. All your cares leave you as you are floating, floating with the ease of a hot air balloon. You go higher and higher, floating gently, smoothly. You go through a few white clouds; float gently with them. You go higher and higher, and the higher you go the more at ease you feel.

You come to a place that is filled with an endless sea of bright white light. You float into the center of this sea of light. It is all around you. The light penetrates you. The light speaks to you of a love far beyond telling. It expresses to you the love of the Father. Float in the light. Let the light permeate you. As you float in it, as you bathe in it, let the light speak to your heart of the love of the Father. Remain in this light, the light of the Father's love, as long as you wish.

PART FOUR

People and Prayer

RELATIONSHIPS AND PRAYER

Augustine once wrote, "The love with which we love God and love one another is the same love." Mature spirituality involves experiencing God in human relationships as well as in solitude. Prayer that moves us away from people can become escapism. Prayer and people belong together. Relationship is not a means to a goal; it is the goal.

Leslie Weatherhead, the well-known Methodist minister, told this story about the trenches in World War I France.

Two friends in the American army were caught in the muddy hell of trench warfare. They were commanded to charge over the barbed wire; the resistance was ferocious, and they retreated. One of the two friends was seriously wounded and left behind. The other friend, disobeying a direct order from his officer, went after his wounded companion. When he returned to the trench with his friend on his shoulder, his friend was dead and he himself had been mortally wounded while dragging him back.

The officer said, "It wasn't worth it, was it?" The soldier looked him in the eye and said, "Yes, it was worth it, because when I got there he said, 'Jim, I knew you would come.' "

We relate to one another not to win a war, not to implement a program or finish a project, but because it's our eternal calling. Relationship is its own end.

TREASURE IN CLAY POTS

In the midst of the earthy coarseness of daily life, in the midst of their humanity, people can become channels of God's love.

Perhaps they don't consciously know this. Perhaps they are not even outwardly religious people, but they have been to us a sign of his love and a means of his love. They incarnate, enflesh, and make touchable God's caring. Many little saviors have incarnated the love of the One Savior. The apostle Paul, in beginning and closing his letters, often said, "I think of you whenever I pray to God." He could also say, "You are to me the aroma of Christ." That great fourth-century saint, Paulinas of Nola, in a beautiful letter to a friend said, "In your personality, Christ comes to me. I meet him in your person."

We encounter God in prayer and we can encounter people in prayer. When we pray we should not run from the people who make up the fabric of daily living, but take them into our prayer. They are fuel for meditation. They are grist for the mill. Prayer thrives on the horizontal dimension. Like Paul, we can remember people in our prayer, the times of closeness and strength. Remembering brings those healing times into the present. In our prayer we can experience again the people who have been to us channels of God's love. We can practice loving people in our prayer. We can bring hurt relationships to a loving God for mending.

IMAGINATION AND RELATIONSHIPS

It is easy for us to live on a physical or an intellectual level in our relationships. But we often miss the intuitive, subconscious cues that come to us. Imagination helps us transcend these problems and overcome our separateness.

My friend Bill uses his imagination to heal relationships. In one instance, his relationship with his boss, a man fifteen years older than he, was strained. A close friendship was deteriorating. His boss constantly belittled him, and Bill reacted defensively. Cold anger consumed him. Spontaneity was drained from their friendship.

Bill took an hour one afternoon to relax and pray, and in his imagination he went into the boss's office, looked him in the eye, and said, "John, what's the problem?" In his imagination his boss broke down and cried and said, "I'm not going to go any farther in this company. My life seems over. My youth and vitality and potential are all wasted. I'm lonely." These words broke Bill's heart open. He realized that his boss felt like a failure and was crying out for affirmation and compassion.

The next day Bill was met with many of the same belittling comments, but he could look past those to the hurt that caused them. He began to experience heartfelt compassion and sensitivity for his boss. His prayer session had helped him become aware of subconscious intuitive signals. He got to the heart of the problem and now reacted with affirmation. His attitude began to change his boss.

The boss slowly stopped his belittling comments. The two began to have many heart-to-heart talks. The relationship blossomed and became even more spontaneous and alive than before.

SCRIPTURE JOURNEY

In the following passage, Paul shows his vulnerability, his need for others. He is willing to express emotions that show his raw neediness, and he does not fear letting people hear of his inner hurt. Part of learning the healing power of community is sharing our vulnerability; only as we share our innermost needs are we able to truly comfort one another.

Do your best to come to me soon. For Demas, in love with this present world, has deserted me and gone to Thessalonica; Crescens has gone to Galatia, Titus to Dalmatia. Luke alone is with me. Get Mark and bring him with you; for he is very useful in serving me. Tychicus I have sent to Ephesus.

(2 TIM. 4:9–12)

Think of a time when, like Paul, you were very vulnerable—when your raw emotions of neediness for God and your sisters and brothers was expressed. Think of a time when you expressed those emotions and people responded warmly to your expression of need.

Now, remember a time when someone expressed his or her inner neediness to you, and you greeted that expression with love and comfort. What did this feel like?

18

TAKING PEOPLE INTO YOUR PRAYER

J eff and Rachel had made it. They lived in a huge, five-bedroom house in the best part of town. Jeff was a contractor who loved his work. He not only made profits on his projects, he made them works of art. Buoyant, always confident, he seemed consumed by his work. He exuded constant excitement, at least on the surface.

His wife was a different story. Rachel seemed quiet; the dark rings under her eyes stared out at you. Her face was clouded with uneasiness. On one of the few days that Jeff was home early enough for supper with her, she sat him down and shocked him with the news that she would be seeking a divorce. She told him that she no longer had a role in his life, that he treated her as secondary, and that she felt ignored. Her complaints were typical of those who are not affirmed and treated as full persons. At one time she had had a career as a guidance counselor in a school. But they made it in such a big way financially that she stayed home to be with the children. Now the children were grown and Jeff had little time for her concerns, no time for their life together.

As Jeff listened he clutched the arms of his chair, his stomach clenched tight with an icy fear. Alone a day later, out of desperation he began to pray. He remembered some of the ways of prayer and meditation that he had been learning from his church. He put on music and lay down on his bed, letting the gentle melody absorb some of the hurt he felt. As a stillness came over him, he took time to remember; he recalled the struggles he and Rachel faced when they were young, the giddy joys, the financial hurdles they had overcome together, their closeness.

For several days in a row he took time for prayerful remembering, and gradually a change came over him. His prayer melted away much of his defensiveness, his armor, the need to be right. He did something unusual for him. He admitted that most of Rachel's complaints were true. He had failed her. His eyes bordered with tears, he asked Rachel to forgive him. Out of his heart he said, "I want it to be like those early times again. And I know I have ignored you."

All of this stunned Rachel. She couldn't remember when she had seen him so defenseless, so vulnerable—it warmed a bit the coldness in her heart toward him. And the strength of the memories that he shared evoked the warm feelings of their early marriage. By telling her what he experienced in meditation, he called her into the experience. She began to weep, too, and a stillness came over them, a quiet full of comfort. Somehow they knew they would make it. They would have a lot of work to do for their marriage to thrive again; the path ahead would be hard. But they also knew that they possessed the strength of many beautiful memories. And they knew that they had God's love; the God who was so much a part of their beginnings was there with them now. That day was the beginning of healing for them.

PRAYER EXPERIENCE

Relax, be still. Go back to your childhood. Let there emerge into your consciousness scenes where you felt loved by another person. Who was it? Remember how that person looked: face, body, clothing. Recall the scenes, the sights, the smells. Relive.

There are also people in the here and now who are channels of grace for you. Imagine someone in your life right now to whom you are close. In your imagination, go to that person at work, at home, at the rectory or convent, wherever you think that person might be. In your imagination, look him or her in the eye. Experience your friend's strength and affection. Embrace that person and feel the warmth of the embrace. Say the loving and affirming things you would like to say in real life, but don't always think of.

SCRIPTURE JOURNEY

According to the Gospel writer, the disciple whom Jesus loved rested on his bosom at the Last Supper. He alone among those who followed Jesus stood beneath the cross. And to him Jesus entrusted the care of his mother. The beloved disciple probably experienced such closeness with Jesus many times, and these bright memories became like a beaded necklace that he could finger and call on for the rest of his life.

One of his disciples, whom Jesus loved, was lying close to the breast of Jesus. . . . When Jesus saw his mother, and the disciple whom he loved standing near, he said to his mother, "Woman, behold, your son!" Then he said to the disciple, "Behold, your mother!" And from that hour the disciple took her to his own home.

(JOHN 13:23; 19:26–27)

Think of some painful moment in your life, a time when you felt alone. Go back there in your imagination. Experience the sights and tastes; feel the feelings.

Now let the adult in you, the person you are now, take that child gently by the hand, embrace that child warmly, and then take that child to Jesus who is standing nearby. Jesus embraces the child, letting the child that was you recline like the beloved disciple on his breast. Tenderness, melting compassion, and comfort rise up within you. This is a memory that you, like the beloved disciple, can now draw upon for the rest of your life.

19

PRAYER THAT HELPS WITH EVERYDAY LOVING

Just as other people channel God's love to us, so we can be channels of God's love to others. The fruit of prayer is not beautiful religious experiences while we pray, though if those happen they should be received with gratitude. The true fruit of prayer comes in everydayness.

PRAYER EXPERIENCE

Think ahead about tomorrow. Go over your day—getting up in the morning, work, school, whatever. Let some scenes and some of the people that might be in those scenes flash through your mind.

Now replay some of those scenes you've just imagined. This time you're going to love the people you meet in the scenes the way you would like to love them. See yourself as a channel of God's presence, a manifestation of his love, his hands, his feet. Love as you would like to love. Care as you would like to care.

Perhaps you're a person who is shy and never talks much. In your imagination, go a little bit more outside yourself to love people. Perhaps you talk too much and dominate conversations. Picture yourself being a better listener.

Picture other ways of loving. And week by week you'll find yourself a more caring person. But don't be disappointed if you don't love as well in reality as you do in your imagination. Remember we are those clay pots that Paul spoke about; the treasure we possess is in those clay pots.

In going through this prayer experience you have no doubt

become aware of ways that you fail in loving. One of the reasons we feel pain, tension, and guilt in our relationships is that we expect far too much of ourselves, far more than God does. His call to us is to relax and allow his transforming love to make us channels of his love. How well he understands that our capacity to love others is imperfect. How much he forgives us when we fail by not loving others as we should. Pause a moment and allow God's forgiveness to flow over hurt places inside you, the places in which you feel failure for not loving as you would like.

20

THE POWER OF AFFIRMATION

How many times have you heard the phrase, "To love others you must learn to love yourself"? Most of us have heard this so many times that it has become a cliché. Many of us have found that loving ourselves is not an easy matter!

A key part of loving ourselves is seeing our inner goodness, learning to affirm ourselves. Many times we are overcome with self-criticism, self-doubt, and fear. At times these emotions paralyze us. Learning to affirm ourselves is a key to establishing strong loving relationships with others.

Our self-image, that is, how we see ourselves, how we feel about ourselves, is often complex and multifaceted. Affirmations and creative visualization are wonderful ways of creating a more positive and loving self-image.

The following prayer experience is one to help you grow in the art of loving yourself. It is often easy to appreciate the good qualities in others and to see their faults and shortcomings in perspective. We are usually harder on ourselves.

Loving yourself can work wonders in your life.

PRAYER EXPERIENCE

Take time to relax and be still. Then review your day so far. Or if it's morning, review yesterday. Think about how you felt at different times during the day. Just notice what ideas and images you held about yourself at different times. See if you notice overly critical, harsh judgments about yourself. Notice their power to ensnare you and to harm you.

Picture a helium balloon whose gondola is a big trash can. In your imagination take these harsh judgments of yourself—as though you were pulling them from your stomach or chest area—and deposit them in the trash can, one by one.

Now take a knife and cut the ropes that are holding down the trash can and the balloon and see those harsh self-judgments float away. Feel yourself feeling light and joyous as they float away.

Imagine that you are in an everyday situation. Someone comes to you with a look of love and affirmation to tell you something very good about yourself. More people join in. They tell you how much they like you and what a good person you are. Soak in what they say. More and more people come and look on you with love and respect in their eyes. What sort of good things do they say about you?

Rest now. Rest a moment in the sense of self-worth that you feel, realizing deeply that God made you and that he made you good.

21

AFFIRMING OTHERS

Mark Twain once said, "I can live two months on one compliment." Mahatma Gandhi, who inspired millions of people to go beyond themselves and accomplish unheard of feats, mastered the art of affirmation. Louis Fischer, one of Gandhi's biographers, gives a clue to Gandhi's ability to transform people: "He refused to see the bad in people. He often changed human beings by regarding them not as what they were but as though they were what they wished to be, and as though the good in them was all of them."

Perhaps the greatest key to enjoying friendship and love from others is warmly and honestly telling them about the beauty we see in them. The open expression of genuine emotion can unlock many new doors for friendship and relationship.

PRAYER EXPERIENCE

Relax. Now allow different people in your life to emerge into your imagination, one at a time. Look into their eyes. Be aware of the goodness you see in them and tell them. What change does your telling them make in the look on their faces? Be aware of how it affects their relating to you. Notice the effect on your own heart of this open, beautiful honesty. Be still and rest in this good feeling.

SCRIPTURE JOURNEY

In the following passage, Paul encourages the people in the church at Philippi, and he lets them know that he also remembers and affirms them in his prayer. For your scripture journey, do what Paul did.

I thank my God in all my remembrance of you, always in every prayer of mine for you all making my prayer with joy, thankful for your partnership in the gospel from the first day until now. And I am sure that he who began a good work in you will bring it to completion at the day of Jesus Christ. It is right for me to feel thus about you all, because I hold you in my heart, for you are all partakers with me in grace, both in my imprisonment and in the defense and confirmation of the gospel. For God is my witness, how I yearn for you all with the affection of Jesus Christ.

(PHIL. 1:3–8)

Picture yourself affirming other people in your prayer in the same manner as Paul. Think about how God's grace has touched them. Experience the goodness that God has poured into them. Let yourself yearn deeply for the completion of their journey in God's grace.

22

HEALING RELATIONSHIPS

Long ago a farmer transported his produce to market in one long haul. His steady horse faithfully pulled the loaded wagon. Each year he added more produce to the wagon as his farm prospered. Then one year his horse keeled over on the way to market. The burden laid on the horse had grown so large that he dropped dead.

So many human relationships are like this. We pile load after load on the people we love till the relationship dies. Perhaps a marriage ends or grows icy cold. Or a friendship dies and we hide our eyes when we run into our friend at the grocery store or shopping mall. We despair of being close to others again.

In relationships we often pile emotional load after emotional load on one another. One way we burden one another is by possessiveness. Each of us has a Grand Canyon of need for love. We easily clutch and cling to others in an attempt to meet that need. Neither husband nor wife, friend nor relative can fill that need—only God can fill it.

Possessiveness does not allow the other person to be free. We love others not for themselves but because they fill a need. A classic example of possessiveness is found in Henrik Ibsen's *A Doll's House*. This play is set in nineteenth-century Norway. The husband is well-off, accomplished in his profession. He keeps his beautiful wife at home where he pets her, pampers her, gives in to her every whim, and expects her to keep the house nicely while he is busily preoccupied in his own world.

He is shocked one day when his wife announces she is leaving him. He begs, he cries, he pleads saying, "Look what I've done for you!" She replies, "No, I'm a doll in a doll house. And you have not allowed me to be a real person. I have faults, I have dreams, I have visions, I have interests, I have things I want to accomplish and you have made me into a doll in a doll house and we have raised doll children."

How easily we can treat one another like dolls in a doll house. We chisel the other person to the shape of our need and then fit him or her into our world. Genuine Christian love allows others to be themselves; it treasures uniqueness. We are bonded together in love and commitment while remaining ourselves.

We have all tasted the pain of having others chisel away at our uniqueness and we have chiseled at others.

SEEING THE WORLD THROUGH OTHER PEOPLE'S EYES

A central way of healing relationships, of loving the way God loves, is to see things from other people's point of view. That's what God did in Jesus. He became incarnate, one of us. The Word became a human being. The second chapter of Philippians says that God did not stay in his lofty estate but became what we are, taking on human form as a servant. Hebrews says that Jesus was tempted in all the ways that we are, except without sin.

To know someone is to love them. God is able to love us because he feels what we feel. He sees what we see. He has walked in our moccasins for awhile.

Each of us perceives the world differently. Some of us perceive the world primarily through thinking, others through intuition, others through sensation. Often our failure to understand others is our failure to understand different personality types. And because different people see reality differently—approach the world differently—we build up walls and fail to love them.

The following prayer experience is an incarnation experience. It is designed to help you know and love others more deeply.

PRAYER EXPERIENCE

In time you will find this to be an extremely rewarding experience. As with all prayer, it takes practice. Deep in our hearts we know intuitively what makes our friends and loved ones tick. It is simply a matter of allowing ourselves to be in touch with that part of us that knows. Relaxing helps profoundly, too.

Choose a person. Remember you can choose a different person each time if you wish. You are going to go through this person's day. Imagine this person when he or she wakes up in the morning, eats breakfast, gets ready for work or school. Get inside this person and feel and sense the world as he or she senses and feels it. Go with this person to the different things he or she might be doing and imagine what this person is feeling. Experience this person's feelings of success or failure. Feel the joys and tensions that this person feels. What are his or her hopes and dreams? See this person with family and friends. Feel what he or she would be feeling.

SCRIPTURE JOURNEY

In the second chapter of Philippians, Paul calls on the people of Philippi to love one another, to be of one accord and one mind. He uses the example of Jesus Christ, who empties himself, taking on our interests and concerns. This is a powerful message about how to get along with people and about how to let love take on flesh and blood in the midst of daily living. Read the following passage over several times slowly, just slightly moving your lips. If you find a particular phrase that harmonizes and resonates within your heart, repeat that phrase ever so gently, letting it nest in your heart.

So if there is any encouragement in Christ, any incentive of love, any participation in the Spirit, any affection and sympathy, complete my joy by being of the same mind, having the same love, being in full accord and of one mind. Do nothing from selfishness or conceit, but in humility count others better than yourselves. Let each of you look not only to his own

interests, but also to the interests of others. Have this mind among yourselves, which you have in Christ Jesus, who, though he was in the form
of God, a thing to be grasped, but emptied himself, taking the form of a
servant, being born in the likeness of men. And being found in human form
he humbled himself and became obedient to death, even death on a cross.
Therefore God has highly exalted him and bestowed on him the name
which is above every name, that at the name of Jesus every knee should
bow, in heaven and on earth and under the earth, and every tongue
confess that Jesus Christ is Lord, to the glory of God the Father.

(PHIL. 2:1–11)

Once you've read the passage over, take time to center, to ease
into the calm of prayer. Carry your thoughts back to times when
other people have counted you better than themselves, have
looked to your interests, have really emptied themselves in a self-
less way in order to understand you, to know your needs. Remember the sights, the sounds, and the feelings. How did you feel? Did
this help you blossom? How did they go about it? Take some time
to remember.

Now recall some times when you have acted selflessly, reaching out of yourself to understand others, times when you counted
other people's interests equal to your own. What did that feel like?
How did they respond to you?

Ponder some people who make up your life right now. Are you
going outside yourself to be interested in their interests? To know
what's important to them? In Paul's words, are you "counting them
better than yourself"?

Now form an image of yourself being interested in these people's interests, emptying out yourself. Of course, realize that what
we imagine in prayer may take time to work itself out in our lives.
Be gentle with yourself; be forgiving of yourself. It will take awhile
for this prayer and this imagery to help you love like that. Know that
every step of the way you have the helping grace, the comfort, the
example of Jesus. He is the one who can transform us, so that our
minds and attitudes more and more become like his.

LETTING GO OF HURT

One day, while visiting my parents, I pulled out an old junior high school yearbook. When I came to a picture of one of my teachers, I felt a surge of fury travel up my spine. The hurting memories, even after twenty-five years, flooded my consciousness.

This particular teacher had caught me passing a love note to the beautiful brown-haired girl who sat next to me. I was just beginning to discover girls and I especially liked her. The teacher opened the note and with a knowing sneer said, "Seems like we have a lover boy here." He read the entire note—every florid word—to the class, which roared with laughter. I turned a vivid scarlet, my blood pounded, my face grew hot with humiliation. I think that was the most embarrassing moment of my life. The teacher needled me about the note for at least a week, and by then my embarrassment had turned to rage.

So as I looked at his picture in the yearbook, those old feelings returned. In fact, they had never left me. I had simply buried them away in some forgotten corner of my psyche where they sapped energy and drained away at least some of my capacity to feel and love and rejoice.

That night in my prayer time, I pictured the teacher. I started to say the words "I forgive you," but my heart was seething with white-hot anger and the words wouldn't come out. I knew I couldn't get through this one alone. As I pictured Jesus beside me, I began to vent the torrent of emotions inside me, pouring out my animosity and anger. For several more nights at my prayer time I spoke out these feelings. By the third or fourth

night there didn't seem to be much bitterness left. This time I
pictured the crucifixion. In my imagination, I moved from the
picture of Jesus on the cross to the scene of the teacher in the
classroom. I had acknowledged the fierce fury within me. I had
expressed it there in front of the Lord. As my imagination turned
back and forth from the scene of pain to Jesus, I felt a love
growing in me, a love growing for that teacher. In my mind's eye
I looked at the teacher's face and I saw insecurity. I saw how
young he looked. I found that I could feel the warmth of compassion for him. I imagined the healing light of God's love around
him. I said, "Lord, bless him. Lord, heal him." And I looked into
his eyes and said, "I forgive you." As I did that, I could see
goodness in him, a sparkle in his eye. I went to him in my
imagination and embraced him. He seemed dear to me now.
Warmth and peace settled in my chest. A radiance flowed all over
my body. It felt so good to have let go of the bitterness.

I couldn't have gone through the process of saying I forgive
you without first acknowledging my feelings and letting go of
the resentment and bitterness. I couldn't have worked through
these feelings without Jesus beside me.

For several weeks after this experience, I found a freedom and
joy, a new lightness in my life that surprised me. For over
twenty-five years, I had been carrying this heavy load exiled
deep within me. I felt a profound thankfulness that we don't go
into that "lonesome valley" alone, but that we have Someone to
walk it with us.

One of our greatest obstacles to loving is our failure to let go
and forgive. Holding onto bitterness poisons our health and im-
pedes us from loving people in the present moment. One of the
greatest things that can free you to receive and give love here and
now is forgiving past hurts. The Greek word for forgive is the
word that means "let go."

PRAYER EXPERIENCE

PART I

Relax. Be still. Allow scenes from your past to emerge, scenes where you were hurt. Look at the people who hurt you. Look them in the eye and say, "I forgive you. I let go of the hurt." Take them by the hands gently and tenderly and say, "I pray God's blessing upon you."

Each time you use this prayer experience, you can imagine different scenes and different people.

As some of the people pass before your mind's eye you will feel uncomfortable telling them, "I forgive you." The hurts are held so deeply that it is difficult for you to let them go. The late Anthony de Mello, in his excellent book *Sadhana,* suggests the following way of letting go of deep hurt and unforgiveness.

First, imagine that you see Jesus Christ on the cross. Take whatever time you might need to have a sense of him on the cross.

Now turn to the scene of pain where you are hurt and stay with that scene for awhile. Keep alternating between the picture of Jesus on the cross and the scene of your hurt. Soon you will find your resentment slipping away, and a feeling of peace and joy will sweep over you. A feeling of lightheartedness will overcome you as the image of our Lord on the cross enables you to let go of imbedded hurt.

PART II

This prayer experience is tied in with the preceding one. After all, we not only want to forgive others, we want to see the beauty that God has implanted within them. It is not enough just to forgive. We want to be able to see the person who has harmed us in a new light.

Relax. Be still. Picture in your mind someone who has hurt you. Get as clear a picture as you can. Try to find some little spark of brightness shining through the unpleasant picture of the person you had before. Then have the light from this spark spread out until it covers the whole person and he or she looks radiant and beautiful. Hold the image of this person surrounded by light before you for awhile.

Look in this person's face and see what good qualities you can see there.

SCRIPTURE JOURNEY

One of the most moving passages in the Bible is the chapter in Genesis where Joseph forgives his older brothers who sold him into slavery for profit. Joseph's attitude brings to mind that of Christ on the cross when he said, "Father, forgive them, for they know not what they do."

Then Joseph could not control himself before all those who stood by him; and he cried, "Make every one go out from me." So no one stayed with him when Joseph made himself known to his brothers. And he wept aloud, so that the Egyptians heard it, and the household of the Pharaoh heard it. And Joseph said to his brothers, "I am Joseph; is my father still alive?" But his brothers could not answer him, for they were dismayed at his presence.

So Joseph said to his brothers, "Come near to me, I pray you." And they came near. And he said, "I am your brother, Joseph, whom you sold into Egypt. And now do not be distressed, or angry with yourselves, because you sold me here; for God sent me before you to preserve life. . . ."

Then he fell upon his brother Benjamin's neck and wept; And Benjamin wept upon his neck. And he kissed all his brothers and wept upon them; and after that his brothers talked to him.

(GEN. 45:1–5; 14–15)

Have there been times in your life when you have hurt someone very deeply, and then that person, like Joseph, searched the far reaches of his or her heart, forgave you, and loved you afresh? Perhaps even with tears and tenderness? Let your imagination drift back to those times and feelings.

Have there been times in your life when you have forgiven other people of serious wrongs against you? Times when you forgave and let go of some of the bitterness? There are few feelings as clean and new, as fresh and vibrant as letting go of bitterness. We human beings were made to forgive.

Aelred of Rievaulx once said if you need to correct another brother or sister, wait until you can correct that person with tears. Are there people in your life now toward whom you feel bitter? Perhaps you are even nursing that bitterness. Say a prayer now that the Lord will help you let go of the pain and move on toward the kind of forgiveness that can express itself in tears and tenderness.

If you do harbor knots of bitterness and unforgiveness in your heart, take some time to visualize what warm reconciliation would be like. Imagine the tears, the reunion, the experience of restored love. Imagine a scene as powerful and as warmly touching as the one you have just read from Genesis. Realistically, the relationship may be so impaired that such a scene in real life may not be possible. But going there through the imagination can speed you on your own way toward healing by helping you let go of the bitter feelings within.

24

RESOLVING CONFLICT

One of the reasons we have conflict with people—the central reason, I think—is our need to be in charge, to have power. We all have hidden power needs. Jesus speaks directly to this. His kingdom does not come by power, but through servant love.

PRAYER EXPERIENCE

PART I

Take time to relax. Imagine a person with whom you have conflict seated facing you. Imagine light from your heart flowing to that person's heart and back again. What does this exchange of healing light feel like?

As you are doing this, imagine a blank screen in front of you. See if the problem between you and the other person appears on the screen. What is it? Look at it a moment. Now erase the problem and let the screen be blank again and see if a solution emerges.

PART II

In your imagination, go to the person with whom you have conflict. Find that person where you think he or she may live, work, or play. Look at the person's face. Look carefully. See what his or her eyes and facial expression tell you. Now ask that person, "What do you see as the problem in our relationship?" What response do you hear?

Now ask that person, "How can I love you better? What do you feel is the solution to the problems between us?"

SCRIPTURE JOURNEY

Jesus, knowing that the Father had given all things into his hands, and that he had come from God and was going to God, rose from supper, laid aside his garments, and girded himself with a towel. Then he poured water into a basin, and began to wash the disciples' feet, and to wipe them with the towel with which he was girded.

When he had washed their feet and taken his garments, and resumed his place, he said to them, "Do you know what I have done for you? You call me Teacher and Lord; and you are right, for so I am. If I then, your Lord and Teacher, have washed your feet, you also ought to wash one another's feet. For I have given you an example, that you also should do as I have done for you. Truly, truly, I say to you, a servant is not greater than his master; nor is he sent greater than he who sent him.

(JOHN 13:3–5, 12–16)

You are seated where you are right now. Imagine that your shoes are off and your feet are bare. Someone is kneeling and touching your feet with warm water and a towel. Feel the warmth and healing of that touch. You look and there is Jesus. His hands move slowly and tenderly. What do you feel? Such love has a way of melting any coldness within our hearts. Perhaps this is what you feel as he washes your feet. Be comfortable with whatever feelings you have. Your unconscious knows what feelings to pick up from the scene. Feel only the feelings that you choose to feel. Take several minutes to meditate on this scene.

Now you hear Jesus say, "If I then, your Lord and Teacher, have washed your feet, you also ought to wash one another's feet. Truly, truly, I say to you, a servant is not greater than his master; nor he who is sent greater than he who sent him. If you know these things, blessed are you if you do them."

Now imagine some of the people you meet every day. In your imagination, wash their feet as lovingly as Jesus washed your feet. How do they respond? What do you feel? Are there ways in your life that you can love with the love of a servant?

Now imagine yourself washing the feet of people with whom you are in conflict. What do you feel by humbling yourself? How do they respond to the wet towel touching and washing their feet?

PART FIVE

Sexuality and Meditation

25

MEDITATIONS CAN BE SEXUAL

I wonder how many of you thumbing through this book turned to this chapter first. The subject of sex immensely fascinates us and, if we're honest, also frightens us. All of us are interested in it.

How can sex and prayerful meditation possibly be related, you might logically ask! The answer is simple. Our relationship with God involves everything that is a part of us, and sex is a vital part of us. I am a sexual human being. From the chemicals that flow through my body to the sense of love and beauty of life that radiates in my heart, I am a sexual person.

Too often we tend to take a narrow view of sexuality. We think of it only in terms of physical acts. Sexuality involves much more than just intercourse. Every time we experience the warmth of affection—affection toward God, affection toward friends, toward husband or wife, toward children, toward creation—we experience our sexuality. Sexuality gives us strength for loving. Sexual meditation opens up this part of ourselves to the healing, transforming love of God as it helps us integrate our sexuality with the whole of our personalities. By including sexuality in meditation, we learn to express our sexuality in ways that help God's kingdom be born in our midst.

Most of us have at least some fear about our sexuality. In the period just after our infancy we might have been taught that our genitalia are dirty. In later childhood and adolescence, we might have been warned, over and over again, of the terrible consequences of our sexuality. We learn to be afraid and ashamed of that part of ourselves.

Right along with the message that our sexuality is dirty comes a similar message that can equally cripple us. It's the message that television programs, commercial movies, jokes at the office convey to us—the message that sexuality is a means of using others, a means of dominance, a quick pleasure fix, proof of our liberation, proof of our womanhood or manhood. It's the message that sexuality is so distant from "the real us" that we can engage in sexual activity casually, lightly, without regard for others' feelings, without commitment and caring, without regard of God and God's revelation. Living out this view of sexuality slowly drains us of life and humanity and in the end can leave us as dead as if we were in a coffin.

Both these messages put our sexuality in a separate compartment from the rest of our lives and the rest of our personalities. When we lock our sexuality behind prison walls, we throw the rest of our personalities off balance. When we block off our sexuality, we block off much of our ability to have a loving, heartfelt response to God. We block off much of our ability to lovingly embrace the poor, the lonely, the hurting of the world. As Donald Goergen reminds us in his masterful study of spirituality and sexuality, *The Sexual Celibate,* "Gentleness and tenderness are rooted in human sexuality. Compassion is a supreme sign of a well-integrated sexual life."

WHAT IS SEXUAL MEDITATION?

As we allow the Holy Spirit to purify, heal, and integrate our sexuality, we unlock the prison doors and permit the sensual, loving energy of our sexuality to flow throughout our personalities. As Fr. Goergen puts it: "Sexuality and spirituality are not enemies but friends. A development of one does not mean a denial of the other. Both flow from the innermost center of human life. Our goal is not to choose between them but to integrate them, to be both spiritual and sexual, holy and sensual, at one and the same time."

In sexual meditation we choose this path of integration. Many Christian churches today are rediscovering the positive role sexuality has to play in all our lives. Catechetical material and guidelines today aren't what they were a generation ago. Twenty or thirty years ago, the teaching most people received on sexuality was a laundry list of don'ts. For instance, among some in the Catholic church and other churches, the apprehension about sexuality was so strong that some considered a kiss on the mouth between an engaged couple that lasted over thirty seconds a mortal sin. Some convents even forbade sisters to embrace their relatives or touch or shake hands with fellow nuns. Such teaching can make sick people.

Now the guidelines for the Catholic church and many of the other churches take a very different point of view. We present sexuality as something beautiful and positive, given by God, a reflection of God's own nature; something so good that the genital expression of it should be saved for marriage.

This is a much healthier approach. Instead of constantly haranguing young people with what they're not to do, the churches teach them right expressions of sexuality. They teach them to form warm friendships, to love nature, to experience the goodness of their own bodies. And because of the intensity of intercourse, because the genital expression of sexuality is so strong and powerful, they learn that it requires a commitment that embraces a lifetime—the sacrament of marriage.

SCRIPTURAL ROOTS

This union of sexuality and spirituality is not as modern nor as radical as it sounds. The Hebrews included their sexuality in their relationship with God. The book of Hosea, one of the most fascinating in the Bible, also presents this passionate God. In a story recounted there, God commands Hosea to take a harlot for a wife. And even though she is unfaithful to him, even though she puts on her paint and sells her wares to every stranger along the road, even though she leaves Hosea, God commands Hosea to go out and reclaim her and love her again, unfaithful though she is.

The writer of the book of Hosea uses that story to illustrate how God loves his people. He loves them passionately. They are his beloved. He is a spouse to them. And even though they are unfaithful, his love is faithful. As Hosea says, "Long have I waited for your coming back to me and living deeply a new life."

Though he refrained from marriage and intercourse, Jesus is portrayed in the Gospels as a well-integrated sexual person—gentle, loving, tender, and warm. As Goergen writes:

He touches people physically, psychologically, and spiritually. He has friends—male and female. One cannot underestimate the importance of John, Lazarus, Martha, and Mary in His life. It is in this sense that His sexuality comes through.

Jesus says explicitly that He wants to be gentle (Mt. 11:28–30). . . . He spent much of His time involved with people. . . . He loved little children coming to Him.

MONKS WHO ARE FULL SEXUAL PEOPLE

Some of the most sexual people I know are Trappist monks at a monastery in the South. In private conversations they tell of God becoming the lover of their hearts. They love God with their work; they love God with the prayers they sing every day; and they love God from the depth of being with their sexuality. Two of them I know consciously allow their sexuality to be a part of their prayer. One of them, a priest who has been at the monastery thirty or forty years, takes time in his prayer each day to include his sexuality. He asks God to keep his sexual thoughts pure and chaste. He imagines a fountain of living water flowing throughout his body, healing, purifying, and channeling his sexuality.

Another Trappist is a hermit in his eighties, living in a little hut about a mile from the monastery proper. One of his favorite positions for prayer is lying on the grass. Bathing in the sun he experiences the goodness of his whole body, the goodness of his whole being. He feels the totality of his whole person loved by God.

A Word of Caution

Integrating our sexuality is a challenge, a beautiful challenge. Yet, as with every important challenge, there is room for caution.

While we are positive about our sexuality we must also be realistic. Sexuality is a powerful force that can take us over and this must always be kept in mind. Yes, it is beautiful and good. Yes, it is power for loving and compassion. But even as we awaken, channel, and integrate our sexuality, we must be careful not to use that integration as an excuse for license.

In Scripture and tradition, God speaks a deep and personal yes to our sexuality. But within that yes are some very clear no's and those no's are for the sake of the yes. Genital sexual expression is limited to the lifetime committment of marriage. Genital expression outside of marriage is inconsistent with Christian moral teaching and holds the potential for emotional, spiritual, (and especially these days) physical disaster.

26

THE TRANSFORMATION OF OUR SEXUALITY

A major step in our journey into wholeness, our journey deeper into God's love, is the transformation or sublimation of our sexual energies.

The people of prayer in the history of the Church speak of God becoming their "Beloved," even their "Lover." They use phrases such as "spiritual marriage" and "spiritual espousal" to describe their sense of oneness with their Creator.

Many like Francis equally know that same "gentle" passion toward people—the poor, the lepers, the wounded of this world. The pictures of St. Francis kissing the sores of a leper and finding in the action a profound sweetness; the image of Mother Teresa tenderly washing the limbs of Calcutta's dying, rapt in loving attention—these show the power of a transformed sexuality. As a famous psychologist of spirituality, Roberto Assagioli, has written in *Psychosynthesis:*

The love energy derived from sexual sublimation . . . extends in concentric circles or spheres, encompassing ever larger groups of human beings. In the form of compassion it is poured upon those who suffer. . . . Finally, it can reach out further until it radiates as brotherly love upon all human beings and upon all living creatures.

All too often when we think of the sublimation or transformation of sexuality we think of someone who has chosen celibacy or of a single person who for some reason has not married. In reality, many who have had the most profound transformation of their sexuality and are full of tender passionate love for God and people are married and enjoying a full sex life. The experience of the transformation and sublimation of sexuality is open to all—celibate, married, and single. Despite the norms of today's culture, sublimation is not a dirty word.

Assagioli compares this transformation of our sexuality to the regulating of the waters of a great river. Regulation prevents flooding and the formation of unhealthy marshes. A part of the water flows through the hydroelectric dam to its natural destination. The channeling of the flowing water produces electricity that brings light and power to thousands.

So it is with our sexuality. When we leave it untransformed and unchanneled it can lead to floods and unhealthy marshes. Rightly channeled, it can be sublimated into power for lighting and healing the hearts of many. And still, in the case of married people, a proper amount can flow to its natural destination, marital intercourse.

This channeling or transformation of our sexuality that comes from our closeness to God and people changes our desires. We see the beauty of God's love in sexually attractive persons. Rather than wanting to consume, possess, or exploit them, we see them as gentle channels of God's presence; we look upon them with a contemplative gaze. St. John Climacus, an early father and saint, describes this:

A certain man, seeing a woman of unusual beauty, glorified the Creator for her, the mere sight of her moved him to love God and made him shed a flood of tears. It was indeed astonishing to see how what for another could have been a pitfall to perdition was for him the supernatural cause of crown of glory. If such a man, on similar occasions, feels and acts in the same way, he is risen, and is incorruptible, even before the general resurrection.

FIRE—A SYMBOL OF TRANSFORMATION

Among many spiritual writers in the Christian tradition, fire is a symbol for the love of God that transforms our sexuality and our emotions. St. John of the Cross sang of "the living flame of love that deeply wounds me in my deepest center." Fire is often the symbolic description of the transformation of sexual energies into strength for tender love of God and others. Richard Rolle was a fourteenth-century man of prayer who left volumes on the experience of prayer. He loved people and laughter and devoted his whole life to prayer and hospitality. One of his prayers beautifully describes this transformation process:

> O everlasting Love, enflame my soul with the love of God, so that nothing save His embraces may set my heart on fire. . . . Enter my heart and fill it with thy sweetness. . . . Burn up my inward parts and all my heart with the fire that burns forever on Thine altar . . . come, most sweet and most desired. Come, my Love who art my only comfort. . . . Enflame with thy fire all my heart; enlighten my innermost parts with Thy radiant light; feed me with Love.

The journey toward greater intimacy with God and greater closeness with people naturally brings about a gentle transformation of our sexuality. Including our sexuality in our meditation can make us aware of the process and help speed it along.

Our emotions tend to be centered in different parts of our body. The word *heart* is used for emotions of love while our spine, our genitals, and the part of our trunk below the rib cage are associated with sexual emotions. This is the area the Old Testament refers to as the loins. It was an area full of important emotions and often associated with the heart. Many ancient traditions consider this area sacred. In *The Experience of Inner Healing*, Ruth Carter Stapleton writes:

> It is significant that the ancients described the genital area of the human body as the sacral area. The words "sacral" and "sacred" come from the identical root word meaning "of Divine origin," "devoted to God." Sexual energies, when first blossoming within the body, cause the transformation of a baby-fat boy into a sturdy man, a gawky, angular girl, into a lovely, appealing woman. . . . Ultimately, this basic drive is the power of God. With this understanding we are able not only to live

comfortably with our sexuality but to be grateful for it. We can give thanks that we will grow and mature to the place where it will be the power motivating us to highest creativity.

The following "sexual meditation" is one way of including your sexuality in your prayer. It uses the fire imagery of Rolle, Wesley, and many others to transform and bring up sexual energy from the "loin" area to the heart. If your imagination is fuzzy, you might look at a candle flame for a few minutes before beginning to implant the imagery deep in you.

PRAYER EXPERIENCE

PART I

Sit or lie down comfortably. Relax. Take some silent time for God to love you.

Imagine a beautiful blue or orange flame (if your imagination is fuzzy today, having a sense of it is enough). This flame begins two or three feet below your spine, encompasses your whole body, and comes to a point above your heart. The flame is the loving presence of God's love. It fills your whole body, burning away fear, negativity, bitterness—transforming them into love and compassion. Feel the sweetness of the flame. The flame transforms and purifies your sexual energies. Feel the flame moving the sexual energy of your lower trunk to your heart. Your heart burns with a newfound love and compassion.

PART II

After completing Part I, imagine yourself loving with a new tenderness the people in your life you are called upon to love. Imagine yourself entering into your creative tasks with a new strength, a new creativity, a gentle and powerful passion. In your own words ask God to continue to transform your sexuality and integrate it with the whole of your personality.

SCRIPTURE JOURNEY

In the following scene from the gospel of Luke, we see a radiant expression of sexuality that's rooted in our tenderness toward other human beings, male or female. The woman tenderly caressed Jesus' feet and kissed them with her hair and her lips. And Jesus allowed himself to be touched and his heart to be melted by this. Although Jesus was never married and never had sex, he was certainly a sexual person. His sexuality was expressed through friendships with people like Lazarus and the women who followed him. It was a healthy, whole, and full sexuality boldly manifested in outgoing love.

And behold, a woman of the city, who was a sinner, when she learned that he was at table at the Pharisee's house, brought an alabaster flask of ointment and standing behind him at his feet, weeping, she began to wet his feet with her tears, and wiped them with the hair of her head, and kissed his feet, and anointed them with the ointment.

(LUKE 7:37–38)

PART I

Imagine that you are the woman who is anointing Jesus' feet with ointment and with tears. Tenderly caress and kiss his feet. Feel only the feelings you choose to feel. It might be tenderness, tinged with joy. Feel this tenderness as a small spiral spinning around you, flowing out to those in need. Picture yourself loving other people with the same tenderness, especially those whose poverty and pain are all too real.

PART II

Unless, on some level, we imagine and practice what Jesus would do, how can we follow in his steps and take on the mind of Christ? So, imagine that you are Jesus and that your feet are being anointed and kissed tenderly. How do you feel?

Now feel this tenderness like a small spinning spiral surrounding you, flowing out to those who need that love. Picture yourself loving others with the same tenderness, especially those who suffer poverty and pain.

27

REPROGRAMMING OUR SEXUALITY IN LIGHT OF GOD'S LOVE

Jake was tall and blond and his well-proportioned muscles told me he was an athlete—a marathon runner, I later found out. It was clear that he was very bright, too. A freshman in college, he manifested none of the confidence I would have expected from someone like him. He was painfully timid; sometimes just a friendly question or hello caused his eyes to dart with hesitation and caution. His walk was uneven. His hands tensed in his lap. Saturday night, after the last session, he stayed behind as the room emptied. As I was gathering up my notes, he shuffled toward me.

"Can we talk?" he stumbled with his words. "I won't take much of your time," he added apologetically. I mustered up all the warmth I could and said, "Of course. Let's go sit down here in the corner." His first words were, "I'm a terrible sinner." I knew that there was more, and I tried with my eyes and body language to let him know that it was safe for him to say whatever needed to come out. Finally, in halting words with downturned eyes, he poured out his story.

When he was twelve, his mother developed multiple sclerosis. As an only child, it was a fearful time for him. The neighbor across the street, a married woman of thirty, came over often to help and often invited Jake to her house to watch TV. This became a good way for him to escape the pressures at home. But then the next-door neighbor began to shower him with unhealthy affection and through emotional manipulation and guilt, pushed him into a total sexual relationship with her, a relationship that smothered and suffocated him. Any time he started to draw away, she would threaten to kill herself. He blamed himself, thought himself to be a terrible sinner. Even though no one knew, he felt a stinging and weighty shame that caused him to withdraw from his peers and made him afraid of any relationship, afraid that in any relationship he would be smothered.

After listening for a long while, I said, "I'm going to tell you something and I want you to trust me. Jake, you were a victim. No twelve-year-old child bears the blame for entering into a sexual relationship with a thirty-year-old. Jake, just let that seep into you." Slowly and gently, the tears came. I sat there with him as he wept. A deep and radiant silence poured over us. I turned on some of the music that we had listened to during the meditations. We tasted God's nearness. I felt it and I knew he felt it. We sat there together for twenty minutes, aware of the gentle, tender embrace of God's caring enveloping the room, enveloping us both. As I glanced at Jake, I could see the warmth dissolve away his tension. He opened his eyes and they glistened this time. "As we prayed," he said, "I felt as though I were surrounded by an incredible light and an incredible warmth. It was like my whole body was made of the light and love."

I looked at him and just said, "Peace be with you, my friend, peace be with you." The next day I noticed that the caution in his eyes was gone. I had a sense that he was going to get the help he needed to really blossom.

Early childhood and puberty, when we discover our bodies and our sexuality, are times of pain for many of us. Perhaps parents caught us in the act of discovering and experimenting with our bodies, and shamed us. Through one means or another we got the message that sexuality was something evil and dirty rather than a sacred, God-given gift.

In our deep self we carry around with us those distorted memories; and those memories shape our behavior even now, like the huge proverbial boulders under the surface of a river that affect its course and flow. Ruth Carter Stapleton, in *The Experience of Inner Healing,* describes a devout young Catholic woman, Susan, afflicted with an enormous amount of guilt about her sexuality in general. She felt that it was something evil and this played a major role in her problem with compulsive masturbation. Of course, the real problem was the enormous guilt and fear of her God-given sexuality. This fear fed her compulsive behavior.

During a conference led by Ruth Carter Stapleton, the young woman went through visualization prayer and returned in her imagination to puberty. She was in her bed, naked, aware of all the changes that were taking place in her body. Jesus and Mary were there in the room with her. They looked on her and saw her as beautiful and good. Mary gave her a kiss on the forehead. She looked up and saw her Lord warmly smiling at her. This and similar meditations helped Susan feel good about her sexuality. Bit by bit the guilt and fear began to drain from her and she began to express her sexuality in higher and more creative ways. Her masturbation problem began to fade as she began to feel better about her sexuality.

The following meditation is designed to implant an image deep within our consciousness of the goodness, the sacredness of our sexuality. In this meditation you go back to puberty and have a beautiful experience of awareness of your sexuality. It's an affirming image, one that can help you experience a great wholeness in your life today. It is an image that can help displace painful and shameful images from those turbulent days of growing up. Some researchers think that a positive imaginative scene vividly imagined can have as much or more impact than real memory.

PRAYER EXPERIENCE

Find a comfortable spot, relax, and take a moment for conversational prayer. Talk with God about how much you need his love to permeate you and help you feel good about your sexuality. Take some time for centering prayer, repeating a short prayer over and over again.

It is a beautiful spring day. The sky is an incredible blue. You are walking in the deep woods. Your nose fills with the smell of honeysuckle and wild onions. You joyfully roll down a grassy hill. You are twelve or thirteen years old. Who were your friends? your teachers?

You walk awhile in the woods, coming to a granite quarry. Large rocks surround a pool of clear water. You sense that no one else is within a mile of the quarry. You're standing on a rock high above the water. You take off all your clothes and stand naked on the rock. You take a deep breath and dive. Feel the cool air rushing past your skin. Feel the cold clear water surround your body as you plunge into the pool. Your whole body feels tingly and alive. You swim to the edge of the quarry, and lift yourself up on a warm granite rock. You take a sunbath, naked on the warm rock. The hot sun beams down on you and reminds you of the love of God. You feel your whole body tingle and radiate God's love. You have a wonderful sense of God in you and all around you. Your whole being vibrates with loving energy. It feels good to be naked. It feels holy. You sense that this new energy vibrating throughout your body will help you enjoy life and help you love.

You sense that a wondrous and beautiful mystery will unfold as your life goes forward. You feel God's presence like you've never felt him before. It's just as if Jesus were standing on a nearby rock looking at you. You feel him that close. And you feel he's pleased with the beautiful changes that will take place in you.

You hear a squawk above you and you look up and see a brown duck, now a flock of wild ducks, beating their wings and flying above you. On the edge of the pool you hear the rustle of grass as a little squirrel scurries about. What wonderful creatures! You wonder at the vastness of the world. You feel a great sense of awe about nature and creation, an overpowering sensation of oneness with the Creator. You marvel at what a unique, beautiful creation the squirrel and the ducks are, the trees that surround the quarry. Then you realize what a beautiful creation you are, too. Your faith is renewed. You delight in the spellbinding majesty of God's world. You become aware of his power within you, and you know that this new energy you have felt surging through you today is holy and good. You have a sense of reverence, that what you have experienced here today is sacred. You decide you always want to use this powerful loving energy in good, creative, and holy ways.

SCRIPTURE JOURNEY

Then the children were brought to him, that he might lay his hands on them and pray. The disciples rebuked the people; but Jesus said, "Let the children come to me and do not hinder them; for to such belongs the kingdom of heaven." And he lay his hands on them and went away.

(MATT. 19:13–15)

In your imagination, return to a scene in your childhood that tended to make you ashamed of your sexuality. (If you were abused in childhood, return to that scene, but only if you are ready.) Once you have returned to that scene, embrace the child you once were. Hold the child tenderly. You know what comfort to give that child; you know how to be tender; you know how to let that child's pain be absorbed by your tenderness. Let the adult in you listen to the child's pain and fear and tears, and hold the child until the child has stopped crying.

Now, gently take the child to Jesus; introduce the child. Jesus takes the child into his lap, and embraces and caresses the child. Tell the child that in Jesus is true safety and true security; his embrace is our true homecoming. Let the child you once were rest in Jesus' lap, cradled in his warm arms.

28

THE MARRIAGE EMBRACE CAN BECOME A PRAYER

I sat in the waiting room at the Atlanta airport nervously tapping my fingers on my lap. My chest ached with anxiety. I was about to board a plane bound for the island nation of Barbados in the south Caribbean. The bishop of that poor country had invited me and a support team consisting of my coworker, Robert, and a married couple to lead two weeks of spiritual renewal in the national cathedral.

To say that I felt inadequate would be an understatement. My failings flashed in front of me like slides on a movie screen. "Who am I," I asked myself, "to presume to tell these beautiful and simple people of another culture about loving God? I feel like I'm failing to love God and failing to love those around me here in my own backyard." I thought of their bishop's great expense in buying our tickets. I was drowning in self-doubt.

Then I heard familiar footsteps coming down the hall. My body began to feel a soothing calmness. I stood up, turned around, and there in front of me were Ron and Ann, the couple who was accompanying Robert and me to Barbados. They looked at me with healing gentleness. Intuitively they knew the anxiety that was eating away at me.

As they both embraced me, the negativity drained from me. Ron whispered, "What a beautiful person you are, Eddie. I know you're doubting that right now, but what a gift you are to Ann and me." As I remained there in their arms for a couple of minutes, a restful sense of my own goodness returned to me. Ron and Ann's love was like a sponge all around me, absorbing my fear and pain.

Ron and Ann are special people in my life. When Ron retired from the Air Force, instead of taking a postretirement job and making a huge income, he and Ann devoted their lives to working with a movement known as Marriage Encounter that helps married couples rediscover the beauty of their marriages.

Ron and Ann's mellow, honest love helps redirect the lives of scores of people—married, single, and celibate. They are frank in saying that they feel that much of their ability to affect others with their love comes from their sexual relationship with each other. They allow their lovemaking to become a prayer. And the gentleness of their sexual union is not just for themselves alone. It flows out from them in the form of a deep-rooted compassion and understanding. Their sexuality gives them the ability to affirm and see the goodness in other people and call other people into that goodness. They take time to pray together daily, time to lovingly share their feelings, to be honest and vulnerable with each other.

The Scriptures of the Christian faith throb with enthusiasm for the sexual genital union of husband and wife. Donald Goergen, in *The Sexual Celibate,* beautifully sums up the attitude of one of the earliest Old Testament writings on sexuality. This is what he says about that early biblical attitude:

There should be no shame about it [sexuality]. It is a gift from God given to man as part of God's creation. Sexuality was given to man in Paradise in order that man should be as God wanted him to be; it is a creation of God . . . sexuality is basically good in that it enables man to be more complete, more as God wants him to be, not alone and isolated but in fellowship.

The part of Scripture that sings out the beauty of the marriage embrace most loudly is the Song of Songs. Its poetry is timeless, passionate, sensuous, bursting over with words like: "How delicious is your love, more delicious than wine! How fragrant your perfumes . . . your lips, my promised one, bestir wild honey" (4:10–11, Jerusalem Bible). The love that the Song of Songs describes is a love that is much more than just physical. It involves relationship. "My beloved is mine, and I am his" (2:16). "I am my beloved's and my beloved is mine" (6:3). It is a love that is committed, a love that lasts: "Love as strong as death . . . love no flood can quench, nor torrents drown" (8:6–7).

BRINGING PRAYER INTO THE BEDROOM

The point of this chapter is that meditation can greatly enhance sex. Even more, sex within marriage can become a profound way of meditation, a profound prayer. Even so, it may well shock you to hear that sexual intercourse and prayer belong together. As an otherwise open friend of mine said when I presented this idea to him, "Eddie, sex is sex and prayer is prayer and don't mix the two."

David Knight, in an excellent book called *The Good News About Sex,* rises to a beautiful crescendo in a passage on the prayerfulness of married intercourse:

. . . [a couple] can mediate and express to one another through their physical gestures in sex the love that God Himself has for them both. God makes their expressions of love to one another His own; what they say to each other in sex, God says. . . . Sexual intercourse for the Christian, is a sacred act from beginning to end. . . . It is an awesome thing to be able to express to another in this way the depth of the passion and love of God.

It is natural that you may feel a twinge of amazement to find intercourse and prayer talked about in the same breath. It is understandable. All of us, regardless of the type or quality of our sex life, still harbor remnants of shame about our sexuality. As you experience more and more of God's presence in your times of making love, those twinges of shame will begin to disappear.

One major problem that prevents many couples from having a deeply holy experience when they make love is that they zero in on goals and payoffs. It's easy to take the attitudes of the marketplace into the bedroom. When this happens, sex becomes merely another challenge. Couples aim toward having better and better orgasms. The loving caresses, the loving kisses that come before orgasm are seen as secondary, a buildup to the big payoff. Instead of attempting to encounter one another in a loving way, they view sex as a difficult challenge, like fighting for a championship.

Another obstacle to meditative sexuality comes when couples hold back their emotions from each other. Having sex with a mountain of unexpressed feelings inside depersonalizes you, dehumanizes you, and leaves you feeling used by your partner. The attitude you take in prayerful sex is the same attitude you take in your private prayer with God. In prayer you come to God as you are, where you are. You come to him without pretense—vulnerable and moldable. You surrender to him in prayer. This lets God do what he wants to do most of all—simply love you. As has been said so many times in this book, you take a sunbath in his love and are healed by his loving gaze.

God surrenders to you; he allows your prayer to touch him. He makes himself so that he needs our love in prayer. God surrendered to us, made himself touchable by coming as a little baby, winning our trust as only a helpless infant can. He surrendered to us, himself infinitely woundable, infinitely vulnerable to us by allowing himself to be wounded on the cross.

Prayer is mutual surrender between you and God. You surrender your expectations, your pain, your fear, your self-hatred; you surrender your concept of yourself before the One who loves you endlessly.

Prayerful sex comes when couples begin to have the attitude toward each other that they have between themselves and God in prayer. Prayerful sex is mutual surrender. As Jerry Gillis writes in *Transcendent Sexuality:* "The purpose of sex is simply simultaneous surrender. Surrender of your demands, of your rigid role, of your ego. Surrender of memory and anticipation. And with all of this surrendering, you will come to know that you really aren't giving up anything at all, but are gaining a powerful new appreciation for the you that really is.''

The Hebrew word for intercourse is *jadoa,* translated in the King James Bible as "know, knowledge." It means more than just our English word intercourse. It means deep, penetrating knowledge, something far more than a head knowledge, a knowledge that goes straight to the heart.

Prayerful sex is living out the full meaning of this Hebrew biblical word. It is a loving knowledge of each other, a loving gaze upon one another. It involves the same type of waiting as contemplative, meditative prayer. You taste the specialness of your spouse. And your husband, your wife, becomes transparent—a window through which you can gaze not only upon the beauty of your beloved, but also upon the beauty of the great Cosmic Lover, God himself. In such a loving encounter you surrender the masks you have developed to keep yourself from being hurt. You surrender your negative programming, and there begins to emerge that unique, loving, uninhibited self, that caring, vulnerable self, that God intended you to be from all creation.

PRAYER EXPERIENCE

PART I

Prayerful sex in marriage is an attitude, not a method or a set of actions. It is an attitude of open loving presence to each other that allows God's love to flow in you and through you.

The following prayer meditations offer ideas that may be useful in allowing sex to be more prayerful. Some of these ideas may be helpful; others may not. Lovemaking is deeply personal. It's different for each couple. Out of the suggestions in the following prayer experience use what is helpful and discard what is not.

Not every sexual encounter between husband and wife can be long and flowing. You just don't have time, especially when there are children in the house. Even though time does not permit every sexual encounter to be long, flowing, and prayerful, everyone does have time for occasional encounters to be planned so that they are long and uninterrupted. Pick a time when you can be by yourselves for longer than usual. When you take special times for slow loving, that experience spills over into other, more hurried times.

When you come together, begin by sharing your feelings and emotions. If you have anger or resentment toward your spouse, get that out. Take time to ask forgiveness and to forgive for any ways you might have hurt each other. Be sure to share positive, upbuilding thoughts and feelings you've had about each other since you last had a chance to talk. Too often we hide the appreciation we feel toward people even more strongly than we hide our anger. Such sharing of the goodness you see in the other person is a way of loving each other into wholeness. It's usually always best to get in touch with the emotions first.

Take time now for silent meditative prayer. It's good to meditate in different parts of the same room. While you are apart, take time to relax; take a sunbath in God's love.

You will be amazed at what a loving awareness you have of the other person in this silent time of preparation. During this period of quiet prayer you might go over some of the other meditations contained in the earlier chapters on sexuality, or any of the other meditations or Scripture journeys. Be open to the Holy Spirit as he leads you. Below are two meditations that you might find especially helpful as you prepare to come together after your quiet time.

PART II

Take time to enter into deep relaxation. Remember. Go back over the many times, the many ways that God has touched your life. Remember your times of experiencing this holy, awesome God of love. Smell the smells of those times, taste the tastes. See the sights again. Let your body experience what it was like to encounter God. Get in touch with the rhythms, the vibrations of those deep experiences when you felt cradled by your Father God. Rest in that love again.

Gather up those experiences in your heart and picture yourself tenderly, without words, conveying them to your wife or husband. Picture the two of you together, tenderly loving each other. Picture yourself caressing and being caressed, kissing and being kissed. In your imagination, let the tenderness of your touch express to your spouse the vibrations, the rhythms of the way that God loves you.

Another prayer experience is to picture your spouse enveloped in the light of God's love. Hold that picture in your mind and gaze upon your spouse surrounded by the healing light of God's love as you would gaze upon a holy picture or an icon.

PART III

When you come together after your quiet time apart, share with each other your inspirations, the feelings that you had in that silent time. Now is the time to begin your loving sharing. Be slow, tender, sensitive; take time for gentle touching. With the tenderness of your touch, express the tenderness of God. And when you are caressed and touched, receive that not only as the love of your spouse; receive it with the same reverence that you would receive the caress of God in the bosom of your soul.

When you are softly joined, take some time to hold one another without movement, maintaining the same type of waiting, loving openness that you maintain toward God in your times of stillness before him. Let the interchange of love flow richly between you. Many couples say that such times of slowing down and being still while connected opens the way for deep spiritual ecstasy to surge throughout their joined bodies and hearts.

And when you are finished, take time for afterglow. Take time to hold one another, to cuddle. Don't rush off.

To close, go deep into your hearts and picture ways that the reservoir of love built up in you from the union you have shared can give life to others: your children, your parents, your friends, and especially those in great need of love—the poor, the lonely, the emotionally handicapped. After looking in your hearts, talk about the ways that you can allow the love you have just celebrated to flow from you to help heal our wounded world. You might close with a prayer of thanks.

SCRIPTURE JOURNEY

These verses, and the whole of the Song of Songs, celebrate the immensely tender, heart-melting reality of marital sexuality. Take time and slowly read these passages to each other.

Let him kiss me with the kisses of his mouth, for your love-making is sweeter than wine; delicate is the fragrance of your perfume, your name is an oil poured out.

—How beautiful you are, my beloved, how beautiful you are! Your eyes are doves.

My love lifts up his voice, he says to me: "Come then, my beloved, my lovely one, come. For see, winter is past, the rains are over and gone. Flowers are appearing on the earth. The season of glad songs has come, the cooing of the turtledove is heard in our land."

(SONG OF SONGS 1:2–3, 15; 2:10–12, JERUSALEM BIBLE)

After you have read these verses, let the tenderness and the melting love they express sweep over you. Sense this tenderness moving around you, surrounding you like a small cyclone of love, as you face each other holding hands. This tenderness, this melting love, summarizes the experience of lovemaking.

Sense the tenderness flowing out of your house to the city, touching those most in need of love, touching them with loving compassion. See the tenderness flowing to the lonely people, the latchkey children, the children in alcoholic and dysfunctional homes, the elderly who are alone. Sense that love going from you, that cyclone surrounding them and imparting some of the tenderness of your own loving relationship with each other.

You Can't Fail

Remember, just as you cannot fail at prayer, you cannot fail at loving sexual union with your spouse. Forget about the past; your aim should be loving and receiving love.

There are dry deserts in sexual sharing just as there are in prayer—times when you don't experience wondrous or glorious feelings. When you feel grouchy, when it seems, at least to you, that something may have gone wrong, those times can be tremendous times of union. Let your weakness show; let your need show. If you accept that and accept that as a gift, such times can bring you even closer together.

PART SIX

Healing Ourselves, Healing Our World

By the waters of Babylon, there we sat down and wept, when we remembered Zion. On the willows there we hung up our lyres, for there our captors required of us songs, and our tormentors, mirth, saying, "Sing us one of the songs of Zion!"

How shall we sing the Lord's song in a foreign land? (Ps. 137:1–4)

The time will come, the ancient teachings say, when the sons and daughters of our oppressors will return to us and say, "Teach us, so that we might survive; for we have almost ruined the Earth."—Black Elk

29

THE POOR ARE OUR HEALING

The TV station flashed 11:45 P.M. I blankly watched computerized information about weather and news pass before my eyes while inside I felt desolate. The week had been especially draining, and I was bathing in a pond of Saturday night dismal feelings.

The phone rang. Some old friend must be calling to have a long conversation! Good, I needed a pick-me-up. I was disappointed, however, for a weak, hesitating voice spoke, "Is Robert there? This is Philip." Robert cherished his sleep and didn't want to be awakened for anything less than the Second Coming. "Sorry," I said. "He's fast asleep."

Apologetically, Philip said, "I'll try to catch him later." I sensed the desperation in his wavering voice. Philip, an old bicycle buddy of Robert's, had been blinded in a car accident six months before. He was calling from the rehabilitation center in Warm Springs, Georgia.

Everything in me wanted to hang up and return to my dismal feelings and the TV set but I stayed on the phone as he gave vent to his sorrow. There had been a misunderstanding with his fiancée. He was lonely. I could hear the gentleness, the openness in his heart toward God and others, and I affirmed that in him. It must have been a thirty-minute phone conversation. We closed and I gently said a prayer for him and led him in a short guided meditation. His weak and wavering voice turned mellow and resonant as he thanked me for listening.

As I sat down in front of the TV again I noticed I no longer tasted my despair. I had been carried outside myself. Remarkably, though it would seem that I was the one who was loving Phil, I think he was the one loving me. He was humble enough to let me encounter his poverty, his need. And his need drew me outside myself—helped me feel wanted. In making myself present to him I found that God, through him, had brought healing to me.

Ten years ago, if I had attempted to write a book like this on prayer, I would have skipped over chapters on justice and peace. For me justice and peace played little role in the real Christian life. All the emotional fireworks of beginning personal encounter with God blinded me to the cry of the poor for peace and justice. It took the pains and joys of aging and maturing over the years to teach me that the poor were a gift, the poor were healing.

Everything Is Related

Often when someone first experiences God's love, he or she tends to view the spiritual life as a roadway to personal fulfillment and a happier family life. While prayer does lead to personal fulfillment, true prayer eventually draws us beyond the purely personal. We begin to see that our individual healing is tied in with the healing of the whole world. Only as I open up myself to the cry of the poor, to their pain, can the healing process begin within me.

St. Paulinas of Nola captures our relationship with the poor in a timeless phrase, "association with the needy which heals our wounds." In short, the poor are our healing! They are our healing because their need for God, their need for grace, their need for love, is up front. How easily we mask our own poverty. Each of us is poor. Each of us is broken. Each of us needs God's love and grace. Each of us needs other people. We try desperately to hide these needs from ourselves and from others. Our TV sets, our movies, our material possessions can easily become narcotics that keep us from feeling the very pain and the need that draw us

close to God and one another. That's why we fear the poor—
because their need is so obvious.

The handicapped, the emotionally wounded, those denied
justice, who live in a state of emotional and physical starvation
can't hide their need. If we dare make ourselves vulnerable to
them, their need tears apart our masks and we experience the
depth of our own poverty. Vulnerability to the poor brings a
wondrous grace to us. When our sister's pain and our brother's
pain become our pain, we are drawn beyond ourselves.

Experiencing All Creation

We can easily miss our interconnectedness with all creation.
The native peoples of North America have kept alive a rich sense
of relationship with creation. A brilliant Navajo student left the
reservation to attend university but after three years decided to
leave. His friends were upset, saying, "You have thrown away
your future. You have so much promise. Why?"

The young Navajo answered their questions by drawing two
circles. In one he drew a large person in its center. In the other
circle he drew several persons, several animals, trees, a hill. He
looked to the circle that had only a man in the center and said,
"This is the modern civilized world." Then he pointed to the
circle that contained people, animals, and nature together and
said, "This is the Navajo world."

I am of Cherokee descent and an active member in my tribe,
the Echota Cherokee. The stories of my people richly season my
Christianity. My Cherokee tradition celebrates the interrelationship of everything in creation. An old Cherokee once told me a
creation story that illustrates this. According to him, the Creator's first act was to create a vast spiderweb out of which he
made the universe. He knit the whole universe together by a vast
spiderweb of light.

The Christian faith calls us to the same vision. Ephesians and
Colossians in particular show that God's healing, God's redemp-

tion involves the whole created universe. We are not saved alone; we are not healed alone. We are healed together in community with other human beings. We are saved and healed together with the whole universe. Paul says, "For he has made known to us in all wisdom and insight the mystery of his will, according to his purpose which he set forth in Christ as a plan for the fullness of time, to unite all things in him, things in heaven and things on earth" (Eph. 1:9–10). And again, "He put all things under his feet and has made him the head over all things for the church, which is his body, the fullness of him who fills all in all" (Eph. 1:22–23).

Our earth is a wounded earth. Our addictions have raped our world. Our massive attempts to conquer the earth have scarred creation. As Paul says, together with all creation, we groan for redemption. (See Rom. 8:22–23.) Only when we acknowledge that we are part of the net that binds together all God's creation does real healing flow into our being.

When I am in the woods or on a mountainside, I often remember how much the Cherokee teach the sacred interrelationship between ourselves and all creation. My grandfather used to tell me that in the ancient days, before the coming of the settlers, the Cherokee revered the earth as our mother. She was Mon-o-la, the sacrament of God's presence. If a Cherokee wanted to take an animal for food, he picked one of the smallest and weakest of the herd, so that the others would grow strong. He would have to justify his kill by a prayer to the Creator and ask forgiveness of the animal, so sacred was all animal life to him.

Even in intertribal warfare, killing another human being was seen as an act calling for great purification and seeking of forgiveness. In even the fiercest wars only a handful of people were killed. Such was the value of human life.

In his saga of his early Cherokee boyhood, Forrest Carter, in *The Education of Little Tree,* tells a story that illustrates the way of the Cherokee. It is a story told him by his grandmother. Her father, named Ground Hog, had a special relationship with trees. He could hear "tree thought." His trees were beautiful, and they weren't at all selfish. They allowed ground for sumac and persimmon, and hickory and chestnut to feed wild animals. Then one day Ground Hog saw loggers high in the mountains, figuring out their plan to cut down these beautiful white oaks. Ground Hog said that the trees began to cry.

The lumbermen built a road to bring their wagons into the mountains. The Cherokees protected the trees. At night after the loggers left, the Cherokee men, women, and children dug trenches across the road. In the daytime the loggers would come and fill in the trenches. Then one day a white oak fell across the road, destroying a wagon. After this, the lumbermen stopped trying to build the road and left the white oaks in peace. Then at the next full moon, the Cherokees celebrated. "They danced, and the white oaks sang and touched their branches together, and touched the Cherokee. Grandma said they sang a death chant for the white oak who had given his life for the others."

Meditation for Compassion

I cannot be healed unless I am open to all creation being healed. That opening heals me.

Our society conspires to numb us. We place a high value on optimism, competition, and being on top of things. We hear so much bad news on television that we switch off our ability to feel what we hear. The apostle Paul calls us to weep with those who weep and rejoice with those who rejoice. Unless we are willing to feel the depths of pain, our ability to feel joy and laughter leaves us also. Part of our hesitation is that we see ourselves as breakable. By taking in some of the pain of the world, we fear we would be shattered.

In *Despair and Personal Power in the Nuclear Age,* an excellent book on meditation for social activists, Joanna Macy says,

The pain we feel for our world is living testimony to our interconnectedness with it. If we deny this pain, we become like blocked and atrophied neurons, deprived of life's flow and weakening the larger body in which we belong. If on the other hand, we let it move through us, we affirm our belonging; our collective awareness increases. We can open up to the pain of the world in confidence that it can neither shatter nor isolate us, we are not objects that can break. We are resilient patterns within a master plan.

When we open ourselves to the pain of the world, we experience resilience—a resilience that comes from Christ's love that upholds and unifies all that is.

The following meditation can help you allow painful information to pass through you without shattering you. A saint once said, "Let all sorrows ripen in me." Prayer can help us make rich compost out of the grief of the world. Meditative prayer can expand the breadth of our compassion. We accept the pain of the world and allow it to pass through us.

PRAYER EXPERIENCE*

Relax. Be still. Imagine that you are surrounded by the light of God's presence. An egg-shaped sphere of the light of his love surrounds you. Have a sense of that love encompassing you.

Now allow images of your fellow human beings to emerge—images of people who are hurting, needy, alienated, sick, imprisoned, on battlefields. There is no need to strain for these images. They are already there, waiting to come forward, by virtue of the fact that we are knitted with creation. Let them gather inside you like a dark liquid. Be open to the pain of the universe, the animals, trees, seas, air.

Notice your breathing, your breathing in and your breathing out. Each time you inhale, you breathe in God's love; each time you exhale you breathe out pain. Feel the pain leave you, absorbed by the light of God's love that surrounds. Breathe out your pain, the world's pain that you have taken on. Feel the light of God's love

*This meditation is based, in part, on a meditation in *Despair and Personal Power in the Nuclear Age,* Joanna R. Macy (Philadelphia: New Society Press, 1983).

that surrounds you, supports you and the whole world. Open yourself to the realization that in taking on the suffering of the world with Christ you share in his redemption. "Don't be afraid of the pain; the heart that breaks can contain the whole world. Your heart is large; trust in it" as Joanna Macy puts it.

SCRIPTURE JOURNEY

The Holy Spirit whom the Father will send in thy name, he will teach you all things, and bring to your remembrance all that I have said to you. Peace I leave with you; my peace I give to you; not as the world gives do I give to you. Let not your hearts be troubled, neither let them be afraid.

(JOHN 14:26–27)

And when he drew near and saw the city, he wept over it, saying, "Would that even today you knew the things that make for peace!"

(LUKE 19:41–42)

Jesus is sitting on a hill weeping over Jerusalem, which is below him. And you are there beside him. From the look on his face, from the sound of his weeping, you sense what he is feeling: deep pain, disappointment, a tremendous yearning.

You touch his robe—I wouldn't be surprised if you felt some of what Jesus feels. Your unconscious knows which of these feelings are right for you. Stay there with him awhile as he weeps over Jerusalem, as he expresses his compassion. You sense that he is weeping not just for Jerusalem, but for all humankind, for all the ways we hurt each other instead of healing and reconciling. Feel only the feelings that you choose, only the compassion and care you choose to feel.

When Jesus finishes praying, he turns to you and comforts you, saying, "Blessed are those who weep now, for they shall be comforted."

Jesus touches you, embraces you, and you feel his peace again.

30

IT'S OKAY TO FEEL THE PAIN

Many people say that we should not concern ourselves with actions and prayer that help heal the world and help
bring peace until deep inner healing has taken place in our lives.
I understand why people feel that way. Some of those who take
part in the peace movement or the prolife antiabortion movement appear to need profound inner healing; they seem driven
by anger, overcome with bitterness. Sometimes that bitterness is
outwardly expressed; sometimes it shows itself more subtly in
tone of voice and in tight facial muscles.

Often, work and actions for peace become a catharsis, a
chance to dump out personal pain, bitterness, and anger. The
image comes to mind of a crowd of antiabortion people outside
a clinic screaming "baby-killer," angrily waving signs as though
they were weapons. I can understand the bitterness of the pro-
testers. I share their goal. I too want to see all abortions stopped.
I want to see life preserved both in the womb and outside the
womb. I want to do whatever I can to prevent abortion, but at
the same time, I want us all to help build a caring and loving
world where no woman would want to have an abortion.

I know in my own life, I am prone to bitterness. I find that
when I feel this bitterness, it is a symptom that I am avoiding
entering into grieving for our wounded world. The bitterness
protects me from feeling the weight of pain: the pain of children
who are starving to death; the pain of the elderly who have no
one to speak their names with warmth; the pain of the unborn,
brutalized and rejected before they have a chance to live; the pain
of our earth, whose rain forests are being demolished by thou-

sands of acres a day so that cattle can be grazed for a few years before the land turns into desert, just so a group of fast-food restaurants will have inexpensive ground beef.

I find that when I do decide to enter into the grief, I feel the pain and let it pass through me. Then it is much easier to speak a gentle, honest, and strong word that can help transform hearts—a word that rings so true that people hear it at the deepest level of their beings and begin to let themselves feel the grief. As I allow the grief to go deep inside me, it breaks my heart open and at the bottom of the well of my heart I find hope—a hope that makes no logical sense, a hope that comes from God's everlasting love. Living, vibrant water of hope rushes in at the bottom of the well, a hope that Jesus said would well up into eternal life. Then I find when I speak of peace, when I speak for the rights of both the unborn and the born, I can do so with an ease and compassion that come from knowing that I don't shoulder the burden alone. I share it with God and with my brothers and sisters. And when I speak out after going through this process, hearts are changed. The compassion warming my heart reaches out even to those with whom I disagree, to the very people that I feel share a great deal of responsibility for wounding our world.

A friend of mine, a beautiful blond-haired woman in her late fifties, attended a three-hour prolife rally. After listening to the speakers' words, which were strident and accusatory, she felt tense and irritated. She said, "Eddie, how much better it would be if they had entered into the pain and were standing there in front of the clinic with tears saying, 'Father, forgive them for they know not what they do.' "

The power for transforming our world is finally the power of powerlessness, of weakness—a power that overcomes the princes of this world, that redeems, that transforms. It is the powerlessness of Jesus on the cross, the powerlessness of Mary, his mother, waiting and weeping at the cross. The enormous power of that weakness can transform creation.

A friend, a pastor, was planning a sermon based on the Scripture describing Mary standing by the cross. He said, "Eddie, if Mary were here today, walking around here in the United States, what would she say to the industrial leaders, to the politicians? What would she say to the people building bombs that could destroy our earth several times over, to people looking casually and without feeling at the disoriented and homeless people on our streets?" I could not picture Mary carrying a sign and waving it angrily. I could not picture Mary like some Vietnam-era protester shouting "baby-killer" at young, frightened soldiers returning from war. No, the image in my mind was of Mary at the cross weeping and grieving over the injustice done to her son and over all the injustice that ever has been or ever will be. I saw her outside the missile silos saying nothing, just grieving—the look of compassion on her face saying far more than a hundred thousand fists raised in a protest rally. I saw her weeping outside an abortion clinic and when she speaks, she speaks little and her words are gentle, strong, and honest.

I believe our hearts will never be whole unless we work for peace and justice, just as our work for peace will be barren unless we are open to inner healing. The two are bound together forever and always. A legend of St. Seraphim, the St. Francis of Russia, helps illustrate this. He was a wise man whose heart was filled with love and caring, whose very presence ushered in healing, whose words were like salve to wounded hearts. In the village near his cabin, where Seraphim spent years in prayer, a woman had lost her little boy, her only child. So devastating was her loss that she shut out the pain and every time we shut out the pain, we become unreal and the world appears unreal to us. Rather than feel the nausea that comes when death has reached close with its cold, terrifying intimacy, she moved into an unreality that isolated her from the people around her. Claiming the child was not dead, she went through the village saying, "Surely there is a medicine that can cure him." Instead of burying the boy, she carried him with her, saying to her friends. "You are hiding the medicine from me." Finally a shopkeeper said, "Go see Seraphim, he may have the medicine for you." Her eyes glazed, she went to Seraphim, demanding a medicine for the boy. He said, "Go to the houses in this village and find one house that has not known sorrow, deep tragedy, or loss, get a grain of barley from that house, and bring it to me. I will make a medicine of it and he will be healed."

The woman did as he asked and as she went from house to house, asking if there had been no sorrow, she found no house without sorrow. She heard people's stories of the great grief in their own lives. Gradually, she ceased to feel alone in her pain. She began to feel her neighbors' pain. Her pain seemed less immense to her when it was seen as part of the pain that everyone felt, and she finally could begin to grieve. She returned to Seraphim and said, "I have found no one that has not known tragedy." As she said that, she began to weep for the first time over her son. She was no longer isolated by denial. Seraphim held her for a very long time as she sobbed. And after days and weeks of grieving, she began to feel a glimmer of hope, the hope of Resurrection and Easter faith.

Entering into the pain of others helps us feel our own pain. We can feel it and let it flow through us and then move on to a place of hope. This is why for real personal healing, for ongoing inner healing, we are called to feel the pain of the world and take actions, even very small acts to help others. I feel that even at the very beginning of our own healing, we need to reach out to heal our world—even if it's the tiniest action.

In our prayer for peace, in our work for peace, even the feelings of bitterness that emerge can be a source of grace if we acknowledge them and take them to God, instead of acting on them. Honest acknowledgment hauls us back to a place of grace, a place of helplessness, a place of spiritual neediness. And it's the place of acknowledged neediness that attracts the tidal wave of God's love. Felt neediness is truly the place of healing.

Another mistake we can make is to be so involved with the world and bringing peace to our outward environment that we take no time for our inner environment. When we blend inner healing with the healing of our world, we are speeded along the pathway toward wholeness.

Prayer Experience

As you enter the refreshing rest of prayer, remember a time when you were carrying a heavy emotional burden that weighed you down and when the people close to you helped you beat it or lessened your sorrow by entering into your feelings.

Now remember a time when you had an experience of helping someone bear a burden. How did this help you grow? How did you feel?

Picture Jesus coming to you where you are seated. He takes your hands gently in his. You feel the pressure of his skin on your hands. As he holds your hands, allow yourself to feel the warm, caring love of his heart that comes to you from the touch of his hand. Now hear him repeat the Scripture, "Come to me all of you who are tired and heavy-laden and I will give you rest."

Sense the burdens in your life as heavy lead balls. Feel their weight. Jesus puts a basket in front of you, and you pull the heavy balls from your chest till they are all gone. Notice how much lighter you are. Feel the deep prayerful restfulness of this moment. You know that Jesus has taken your burden.

Jesus takes your hands again. Feel the warmth of his touch. He says to you, "Take my yoke upon you and learn of me for my yoke is easy and my burden is light." As he holds your hands he shares with you, without words, some of his concern, his compassion for the world. Rest a moment with your hands in his.

31

PRAYER AND PEACEMAKING

Harry and Pat came into our lives and our ministry at a time when we deeply needed people to love and affirm us. Harry is a retired colonel, a West Point graduate. Tall and distinguished, he has eyes that show mellow compassion and love. Harry is a straightforward person who tells things as he sees them, but he does so in a way that is respectful of other people. We grew close to him and his wife Pat during a time when I was becoming aware of the enormous pain of the world—poverty, injustice, the holocaust of abortion, and especially the deadly serious problem of the arms race.

The way I reacted to all this pain was to become bitter. I developed a fierce, unruly anger. One night when we were having supper with Harry and Pat, my conversation began to send out not so subtle hints of my anger. I was deeply worried about growing militarism and the heating up of the nuclear arms race, and Harry was the nearest target for my anger. In an obvious, yet indirect way, I started chomping away at Harry. He certainly knew what I was doing. The conversation soon disintegrated into a yelling contest, with me doing the major part of the yelling.

Afterward when I was alone, I felt dirty inside, experiencing that raw feeling you get when you realize that you've been self-righteous. I moved into sorrow for the way I had treated Harry. The memory of his strong, compassionate eyes, his interest in my ministry, and his loving affirmation of my work came to mind. I remembered too how he and his wife were spending so much of their time and energy to help God's people. They lived on their retirement checks and used their freed-up time to help develop our church's ministry to the poorest of the poor—a food bank and an all-volunteer social service center. In addition, they have headed and implemented a parish renewal program that is transforming our parish. It dawned on me that even though I have honest and legitimate differences with Harry on how to bring peace, in his own way Harry is probably doing far more than I am to help the most wounded people in our society. I was beginning to learn a lesson that would take a long time to sink in: uncontrolled anger seeps deep down within us as bitterness, and it undoes our words of peacemaking and our work for justice.

Slowly I began to learn the power of grieving, the power of anguish. In the Old Testament, when we hear the word *prophetic* we often think of anger. But the central characteristics of prophecy, according to the biblical scholar Walter Brueggemann, are anguish and grieving, not anger and bitterness. Old Testament prophets grieved, not out of self-importance, but out of heartfelt compassion. In their grieving they were open to God pouring into their hearts the astonishing hope, redemption, and liberation of his love.

Long before Jesus, the prophets moved beyond the warlike character of early Israel and called for peace. The prophet Isaiah could say, "Woe to those who go down to Egypt for help and rely on horses, who trust in chariots because they are many and in horsemen because they are very strong, but do not look to the Holy One of Israel or consult in the Lord!" (Isa. 31:1).

The Old Testament is oriented not so much to another world as it is toward the future. It looks to God's reign not so much as a where but as a when. All history, all the interactions of human beings, moved toward a time when God's reign would make all creation new. Micah gives an earthshaking description of this coming era: ". . . they shall beat their swords into plowshares, and their spears into pruning hooks; nation shall not lift up sword against nation, neither shall they learn war any more" (Mic. 4:1–3).

This new era broke into the world in Jesus. He brought a way out of the spiral of violence. His teaching pointed to something other than hate producing hate and killing producing killing. He said, "You have heard that it was said, 'An eye for an eye and a tooth for a tooth.' But I say to you, Do not resist one who is evil. But if any one strikes you on the right cheek, turn to him the other also; and if any one would sue you and take your coat, let him have your cloak as well; and if any one forces you to go one mile, go with him two miles . . . You have heard it said, 'You shall love your neighbor and hate your enemy.' But I say to you, Love your enemies and pray for those who persecute you, so that you may be sons of your Father who is in heaven" (Matt. 5:38–45). And, of course, Jesus said, "Blessed are the peacemakers, for they shall be called children of God" (Matt. 5:9).

Jesus calls us to be peacemakers. Christian prayer can lead us beyond just praying for peace to being instruments of peace.

Peace among people and with the whole created world held the highest importance to the Cherokee. Prayer knits us back together with our mother the earth, our father the sky, our grandmother the sun, and helps us see clearly again the stars. We see the beauty of whatever is before us.

My full-blooded distant cousin, Dhyani Ywahoo, dedicates her life to working for peace. A medicine woman who has helped preserve the sacred Cherokee tradition, she and her husband operate a retreat house in Vermont and speak throughout the United States, bringing this bright Cherokee tradition of healing peace to bear on the painful brokenness of our world. In a note to me, Dhyani made a striking statement on peace:

Through meditation, chants, dance, and prayer, one becomes a sacred spindle, to weave anew the web of beauty and harmony. A wondrous tapestry of light unfolds and the vision of peace is made real at this time.

We pray not only that God bring peace but that we be spindles that weave peace—or as St. Francis said, "instruments of His peace."

Violence among individuals comes when we project onto others the things we dislike about our own selves. We tend to see in others the things within ourselves that we have not yet learned to accept and integrate. Usually the things that infuriate us about others are things that are in us. We try to eradicate the things we do not like within ourselves by eradicating those things in others. At the worst level we not only want to eradicate the behavior in others, but even want to get rid of the problem within ourselves by getting rid of the person we project the problem onto.

And so it is with nations. Prayer helps us deal with our inner defensiveness and violence. In the stillness of prayer, deeper and deeper parts of us taste of God's acceptance. Prayer unhooks us from the fears that lead to warfare in families, warfare among friends, and warfare in our world. Prayer disarms us inside.

When we pray, we are put in touch with hope. We savor God's goodness, God's final triumph over the forces of disruption and alienation in our world.

PRAYER EXPERIENCE

Remember a time when you were in angry warfare with some of the people you love most. Recall a time when you were at odds with those around you and others helped make peace among you. What did they do? What did their presence as they were making peace feel like? What went on in you as they made peace?

Now picture yourself acting in a way that helps bring peace to people who are at odds with one another—family, coworkers, friends, people in your parish. Picture yourself making peace. What do you do? What do you say? What do you feel? At what times do you keep silent? Does patience play a role?

Now picture yourself taking some small action that helps bring the world toward peace. Perhaps you participate in a fund drive to help the hungry in underdeveloped countries. Perhaps you write your congressman. There are many directions to take. You may return to this part of the meditation many times before scenes come up that feel right for you. Listening to and responding to our call to become peacemakers takes time.

Now we are moving to an experience of God's presence, of God's hope working within us to make peace. Notice your breathing, your breathing in and breathing out. The word for the Holy Spirit in Scripture is the word for breath. Let your breathing in and breathing out remind you of the Holy Spirit.

Picture yourself surrounded by a sphere of light. Breathe the light in and out. The center of your body glows with that light. Light flows through your entire system, the light of God's presence bringing peace and hope. Have a sense that this light that you continue to breathe in flows out from your heart. Let it surround the building you are in. See the people there surrounded by God's light, surrounded by his peaceful presence. Sense that light coming from him through you to others, bringing them peace and healing.

Think of members of your family who are hurting each other now. Think of some of your friends who are hurting each other now. Picture that light flowing out of your heart to them, bringing peace. Picture that light surrounding your neighborhood, bringing light to those who are tearing one another apart with their words, bringing light to families who abuse one another not only with words but also with violent acts. Picture that light flowing over the whole country, bringing peace.

Picture the light surrounding landless peasants and government soldiers in a Third World country, who are shooting bullets at one another. See that light cause them to drop their weapons and embrace one another. Picture the light surrounding the missile silos and causing them to disappear. See the whole world enveloped in the shimmering fullness of the light of God's peace and love.

Pause for a moment in awareness of the powerful image you have just prayed. In your own words and in your own way, ask God to help you be an instrument of his peace. Pause a moment and see if there come from your deepest self images and pictures that can lead you into becoming that instrument.

Relax, center, be still. Let your imagination take you back to a time when you experienced peace—peace within you, peace with those around you, peace with your environment. Rest in that memory. Feel the feelings again, taste the tastes, see the scenes. Rest in that memory a moment.

SCRIPTURE JOURNEY

And when they came to the place which is called the skull, there they crucified him, and the criminals, one on the right and one on the left. And Jesus said, "Father, forgive them; for they know not what they do."

(LUKE 23:33–34)

Gently now, go to the scene of Jesus' crucifixion. See him there on the cross. Become aware of his suffering, aware of his pain. A feeling of great compassion surrounds him, the taking on of a great suffering. Your unconscious mind knows how much you should enter into these feelings. Picture the beloved disciple and Mary under the cross. The scene takes place not in Jerusalem two thousand years ago, but today. Jesus on his cross faces a vast boulevard in modern times. You are there. Enter into the feelings.

Now you hear sounds, clanking sounds. A military parade makes its way along the boulevard in front of Jesus. Missiles pass by under Jesus, followed by tanks. The loud din of metal banging against pavement fills the air with disharmonious sound. Fluttering high above the parade is the American flag, carried by three soldiers. Jesus notices the parade. What is the expression on his face?

The clanking sounds grow loud again. More tanks and more missiles make their way down the boulevard. This time the flag is red, emblazoned with a hammer and sickle. Soldiers carry a large flower-covered picture of Lenin. What does the expression on Jesus' face seem to be saying?

The parades are finished, the boulevard silent. Now Jesus looks down toward you and gives you a message for the political leaders in the Kremlin. He also gives you words to say to the political leaders in Washington. Picture yourself going first to the leaders in

Moscow, then to the leaders in Washington and telling them what Jesus told you to tell them. What is their reaction? How do they respond to you?

Now it is time to turn your attention to the chair where you are sitting. As you sit there, imagine Jesus coming to you, putting his hand on your shoulder. Your heart may be disquieted after the scenes you have just seen and the words you have spoken to the political leaders. His arms and his love envelop you. Allow those well-muscled and tender arms to bring comfort. Pray this meditation often. Soon you may find small ways in which you can begin to help bring peace.

32

ON THIS DAY IS CHRIST RISEN

When I give talks at retreats, I usually pick out two or three lively faces in the audience—people whose eyes are lit up, who closely follow what I am saying. I find such faces reassuring, and I keep my eyes on them during much of the talk, as if we were having a private conversation.

At one retreat there was an elderly couple in their eighties who showed faces bright with joy, drinking in each word I said; they were very special. It was as if a light came from their hearts to mine and knit us together. I felt this, and I know they felt it too.

During a three-hour break one afternoon, they took me aside and said, "We want to ask you to do something for us. We would like to take a while and talk to you about it." Normally I would have to say no to such a request. I need those breaks to renew my energy, to go over my ideas for the upcoming sessions. But this time, I knew I needed to spend time with this couple. We found an empty classroom away from everyone else.

And then they began to share their lives with me. It was obvious that they were deeply in love with each other and always had been. They seemed like people who had always been naturally good and didn't have to try hard, as most of us do. Love naturally flowed from them. But as with most people who are able to love genuinely, suffering had played a role in their lives.

They told me about their only child, Robby, who had been born right after World War II. The little boy was the sunshine of their lives. They shared stories with me about him that were funny and stories that touched. Robby had died of meningitis when he was six years old. He became sick one day with what they thought was flu, and the next day he was dead. They shared this sorrow with me. Every month since his death, they place a new toy on his grave, and they keep his memory shining bright.

As I listened to them, I found that age had isolated them. The man had no brothers or sisters. His wife had a sister who had died a long time ago without bearing children. Most of their friends were dead. They had no one. And because they were old and ill, they feared both being left alone and leaving the other one alone, since they had known so much caring, so much love from each other.

They looked at me and from their hearts they said, "We want you to do something for us. We want you to remember. When you pray, remember us. And please remember the stories we told you about our son, because we lament that all knowledge of him will leave the earth with us. After we are gone, if you are ever in this part of the country again, if you at all can, please go by his grave and leave a toy."

Without thinking about it, the three of us had formed a circle and put our hands on one another's shoulders. We stayed there for a long time with tears of grief trickling down our cheeks. Their willingness to grieve helped me to grieve over some of the losses in my life. After a while, I said, "Oh yes, I will remember. And I'll tell other people to remember." As the tears ceased, we were enfolded in the heart of God. His heart beat with our hearts; he breathed in our breath. We felt a powerful hope, a powerful joy, an intimation of resurrection course through our arms to one another, slowly rising to a mighty crescendo, a bright astonishing hope that only God can bring.

The faith we have is that if we embrace our anguish, it will not overwhelm us, but the hurt will open us into the astonishing surprises of God. The couple I met had spent thirty-five years not in emotional numbness, not hiding away the hurt, and their lives flowed with the reality of their hope. And my experience with them helped me cope with a profound loss that was to come into my life.

In 1986, my older cousin Billy Joe died suddenly and unexpectedly. He was an only child, as I am, and I had always regarded him as a brother and his parents, Aunt Margaret and Uncle Bill, as second parents. A few weeks after his death, a car accident instantly killed Uncle Bill and left Aunt Margaret seriously injured (she has now fully recovered). In my time of grieving, my faith made little sense for awhile. I felt no comfort or hope. I was desolate. I told my friends, "You will have to believe for me."

The weeks following their deaths seemed hopeless, endless. I was not even consoled by a felt sense of God's presence. I was powerless to hope as an act of my will. Then one day I was reading an old funeral service for children, "The Mass of the Angels." I read the words, "May the angels bear you upon their wings to paradise." The words resonated in the inner chamber of my heart.

Somehow I knew, with a knowing that is beyond words, that Billy and Uncle Bill rested in the bosom of Jesus. I could not have talked myself into such knowledge. That knowledge came as a gift. My whole body was filled with the white light of hope, the hope that only the Holy Spirit can bring. As Walter Brueggemann once wrote, "Our hope is never generated among us, but given to us. And whenever it is given, we are amazed." We cannot produce hope in ourselves; we cannot talk ourselves into it. Hope is like the wind. We can put out the sail and make it ready to receive, but only God can bring the wind.

In going to church, in reading the Bible, and in praying, even in the midst of that dismal time, I was unfurling the sail to wait for the wind. Real Christian hope comes only when we accept the magnitude of the loss. If we hide away the hurt, we close our hearts to hope. It's only as we embrace the pain and the loss that hope can come. After grieving will come comfort; after a night of weeping, joy in the morning; after brokenness, mending; after hostility, forgiveness; after estrangement, reconciliation; after repression and dehumanization, justice; after death, homecoming and resurrection.

In the resurrection of Jesus Christ, the future broke into the present. Jesus fully embraced the heartache of the whole world and spoke a powerful word of newness. His coming is the rising sun that chases all shadows, dispels all doubt, comforts all grief. His resurrection lights up the shadows of our hearts. It brings a love as wide as the earth, as free as the open sky, as deep as the deepest river, as gentle as the spring wind. His rising is the sun that shatters the darkness; it stills the unsettled waters within our hearts; it is the bridge that crosses the stormy sea of our pain, the medicine that cures our hurts. The risen Lord is the calm weather after the storm; he enfolds the universe in his tender mercy. It is, as Karl Barth put it, "the glory of God investing the whole creation . . . of every time and place with unspotted and imperishable glory."

The Holy Spirit gives us a glimpse of that great and coming light. The most powerful sense I have ever experienced was during Holy Week worship at the Russian Catholic church of St. Andrews in El Segundo. The moving Eastern Christian worship does more than read Scripture; it often acts out the events. The worship service tends to be long, and the congregation, many of whom are Russian refugees, is fervent.

On Good Friday we gathered together in a long service and sang mournful music in both English and Russian. At one point in the service, we all came forward to kiss a cloth icon of Christ's body, laid out with all his wounds. We kissed it and took a flower—in a sense, a flower from the funeral of Jesus. The church was darkened, and many of the old women with scarves around their heads had tears streaming down their cheeks.

Then on Saturday night we gathered again. Almost all the lights in the church were out and again the music was mournful. At one point we went hunting for the body of Jesus. The priest led, shaking a censer that gave out the pungent aroma of incense.

Then, at the right moment, the priest shouted out in a loud, triumphant voice, "Christ is risen." I am sure he woke people up blocks away in that residential neighborhood. People threw their arms around one another, kissed each other, and cried, "Christ has risen," to which the response was, "He has risen indeed." We all lit candles, the lights of the church were turned on, and the bells began to ring. We sang triumphant hymns and chanted litanies for several hours more in the church. And when someone felt like it, he would again take up the cry, "Christ has risen." I felt as though I were going through the death and resurrection with Christ. We did more than witness it; we were caught up in it. All of us were dying with Christ and being buried with Christ and then triumphantly rising with Christ. I felt transported to a different place and time. It was the most stirring time of worship and hope I have ever experienced. Afterward, we all celebrated, at four o'clock in the morning, with a huge Russian breakfast. I have never met a warmer congregation.

The following prayer experience is meant to carry you into the darkness of the tomb, into the death of Jesus and into his rising. When I first went through this meditation, I was afraid I was approaching something too sacred. We can watch with the women and John at the crucifixion, but we shy away from the tomb since our culture teaches us to deny death. I also hesitated to carry myself through this prayer experience because I thought that the moment of resurrection was a private thing between Jesus and the Father. But then I remembered the imagery of St. Paul—if we died with him in death, then we will arise with him in new life. Scripture calls us to have the same mind that was in Christ Jesus.

PRAYER EXPERIENCE

In your imagination, you are no longer seated just in your chair but in the darkness of a cave that is a tomb, the tomb of Jesus. You are there with his recently buried body. There is absolutely no light. It is a darkness that exceeds the deepest darkness of the deepest mines. Most of us fear graveyards at night—especially the thought of being in a grave or a tomb at night. Such images convey some of our deep-seated and unspoken terrors.

You know this is Jesus, and you have read and been told that he will rise again. But somehow having been told that, having read that, does not change the dark atmosphere of death, with its finality and its shadowy assault upon our joy and upon creation. There is an unspeakable nausea to death, an utter loneliness. Even the knowledge that Jesus' "corpse," there with you, will rise from the dead does not lessen the overwhelming sense of loss and anguish.

At such times, it is easy to feel all the losses and all the griefs of your lifetime. The tomb emanates a swirl of feelings independent of you. It is as though all the pain, all the sorrow, all the grief, all the God-forsakenness of all creation have been drawn into this tomb. Your inner heart knows which of these feelings is best for you to feel now. So whatever you feel is what is right for you to feel.

Now I would like for you to do something, when you are ready and only if you feel you are ready. What I would like for you to do is reach out and touch Jesus. Slip your hand through the linens until you find his hands. Take his hand in your hand. The knuckles are cold and hard. He feels dead, so very dead. The hand feels stiff like steel. As you hold the hand, I would not be surprised if you find yourself drifting into that state somewhere between wakefulness and falling asleep when we have the first hint of dreaminess. I would not be surprised if some of your personal losses arise within you. Somehow you know that the grief you feel, the loneliness, the utter aloneness, the isolation, the finality of what is here, is the woundedness of creation—not only your own pain, but the pain of the world; not only your own grief, but the grief of the world.

You drift even farther, floating into a dreamlike state of calm and rest—a quietness so profound that it soothes you and comforts you. Slowly the pain and the tension begin melting away. You move into the midst of the gentlest of transitions; a full feeling of grace and ease swells within. The mood begins to change to that of calmness. There is a presence you cannot see, one you cannot hear, but a presence even still. A comfort begins to move in your heart and in the room and in the tomb. A comfort swirls about you, comfort such as you felt as a child when you cried in your mother's lap and she consoled you. A bright light begins to surround you in your dreaminess. You notice that Jesus' hand has become warm and alive. His hand now comforts and warms you. All around you is light unlike any you have seen before. It resembles light, but our word *light* can only hint at it because it is so much more than light. It awakens senses you never knew you had, ways of seeing and feeling that you never used before but that were always a part of you. It's a light beyond light.

Now you are standing in the middle of the light with Jesus. Your hand is in his nail-pierced hand, and you are hovering above the earth. An intense and radiant brightness bursts forth around you, immersing you in a warm caress of tender love; immense and radiant love flows from his hand to yours. A total love, a pure love soothes every cell of your body, filling the inner places of your heart. The brightness bursts out into the farthest reaches of the universe. There is a feeling like warmth, but better than warmth; there is a feeling like joy, but far richer than any joy you have ever known, so that joy does not give it a name. It's as though all the terrors that you felt have melted away into hope, a hope that our word *hope* can only hint at. And love is there. But our word *love* is too limited to describe this love. Your hands and your feet pulsate with warmth, and you know that not only your pain, griefs, losses, and fear, but all pain, fear, and loss are being transformed into this light.

Rest there in the warmth and the light that is full of caring, personal and alive. Stay there as long as you wish and experience the healing.

ADDITIONAL READING

GENERAL

Kelsey, Morton T. *The Other Side of Silence.* Mahwah, NJ: Paulist Press, 1976. A classic on meditation and imagination from a biblical, historical, and Jungian perspective.

Linn, Dennis, et al. *Healing the Greatest Hurt.* Mahwah, NJ: Paulist Press, 1985. A moving, highly practical guide to the healing of the losses we encounter in life.

Stapleton, Ruth Carter. *The Experience of Inner Healing.* Waco, TX: Word, 1975. A book of great depth, practicality, and wisdom—a work of love.

Underhill, Evelyn. *Mysticism.* New York: New American Library, 1955.

White, Anne. *Healing Adventures.* Dearborn, MI: Logos Books, 1972.

RELATIONSHIPS

Powell, John. *The Secret of Staying in Love.* San Diego: Tabor, 1974. Perhaps the best book ever written on how to communicate and share emotions.

Savary, Louis. *The Heart of Friendship.* San Francisco: Harper & Row, 1978. Practical help in the dynamics of relationships.

SEXUALITY

Assagioli, Roberto. *Psychosynthesis.* New York: Penguin, 1971.

Goergen, Donald. *The Sexual Celibate.* Garden City, NY: Doubleday/Image, 1979. The best book ever written on the relationship of sexuality and spirituality. Despite the title, it is full of information for married and single people, as well as the celibate.

Gillis, Jerry. *Transcendent Sexuality.* New York: Holt Rinehart & Winston, 1981. Much practical information, yet written from a secular perspective that at times is in conflict with good gospel and family values.

Knight, David. *The Good News About Sex.* Cincinnati: St. Anthony's Messenger Press, 1980. A practical, moving, and wise view of sexuality. Especially good for young people.

PEACE AND JUSTICE

Brueggemann, Walter. *The Prophetic Imagination.* Philadelphia: Fortress, 1978. This book is a spontaneous act of generosity and love by a world-renowned biblical scholar who writes with heartfelt emotion on hope and imagination. Highly readable.

Macy, Joanna R. *Despair and Personal Power in the Nuclear Age.* Philadelphia: New Society Press, 1983. Macy breaks new ground in the field of grieving over and healing the pains of the world.

Wallis, Jim. *Call to Conversion.* San Francisco: Harper & Row, 1983. Perhaps the best book available on justice and peace from a biblical perspective.

PSYCHOLOGY

Bry, Adelaide, and Marjorie Bair. *Directing the Movies of Your Mind.* New York: Harper & Row, 1978. Summarizes most of the major research on imagination in a popular, readable style. A must book for the serious student of imagination and meditation.

Vaughan, Frances E. *Awakening Intuition.* Garden City, NY: Doubleday, 1979. Another excellent study of the imagination.

GUIDED MEDITATIONS

de Mello, Anthony. *Sadhana: A Way to God.* Garden City, NY: Doubleday/Image, 1984. Wonderful—a classic; emotionally moving, practical, and helpful.

LeShan, Lawrence. *How to Meditate.* New York: Little, Brown & Co., 1974.

Wuellner, Flora S. *Prayer, Stress, and Our Inner Wounds.* Nashville: Upper Room, 1985. A beautiful blend of healing, imaginative meditations, and practical wisdom.

For more information about his series of nationwide retreats and renewal conferences, please contact Eddie Ensley at the following address:

Contemplative Brothers
P.O. Box 8065
Columbus, GA 31908